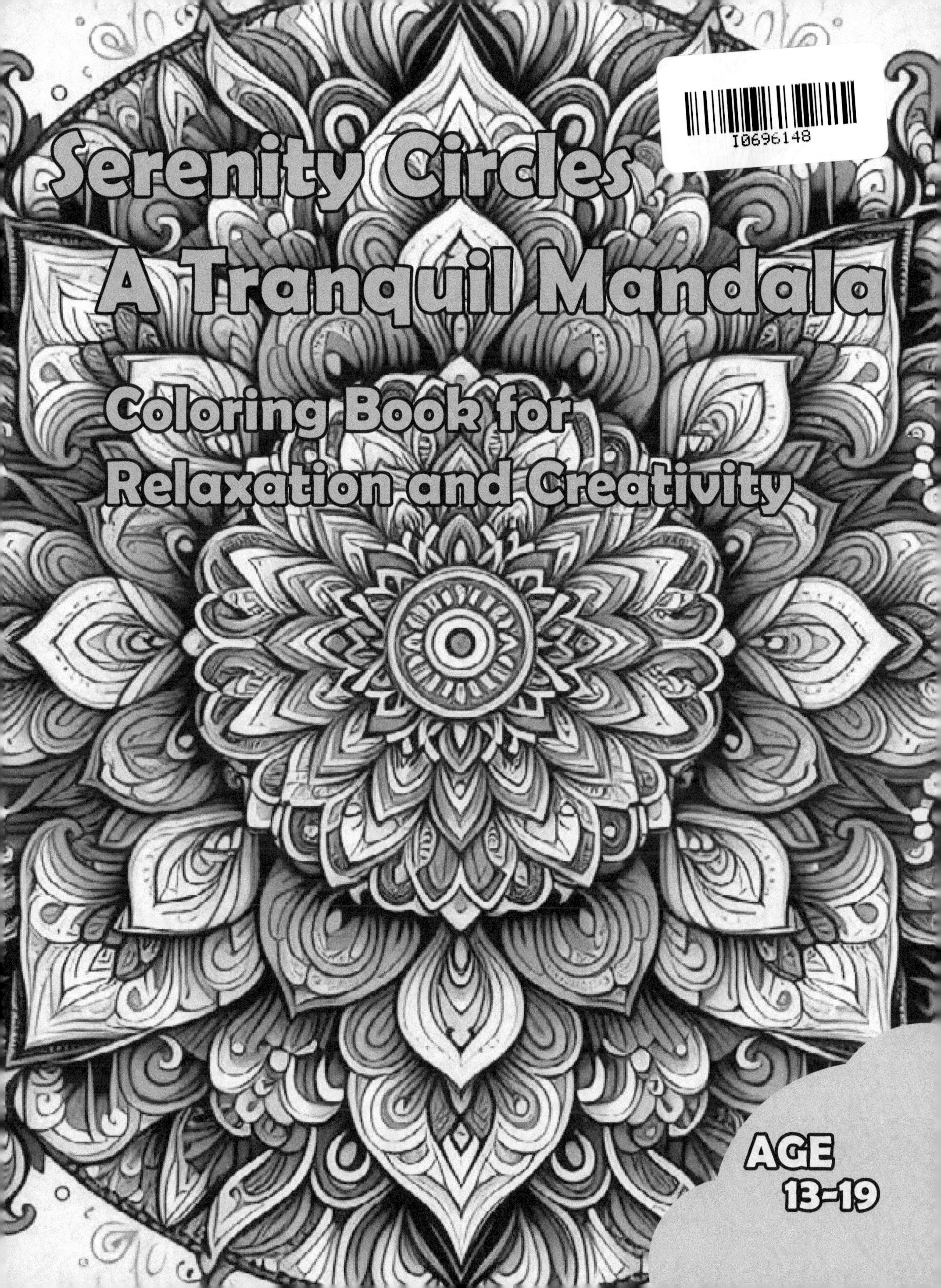

Serenity Circles
A Tranquil Mandala
Coloring Book for
Relaxation and Creativity
I0696148
AGE
13-19

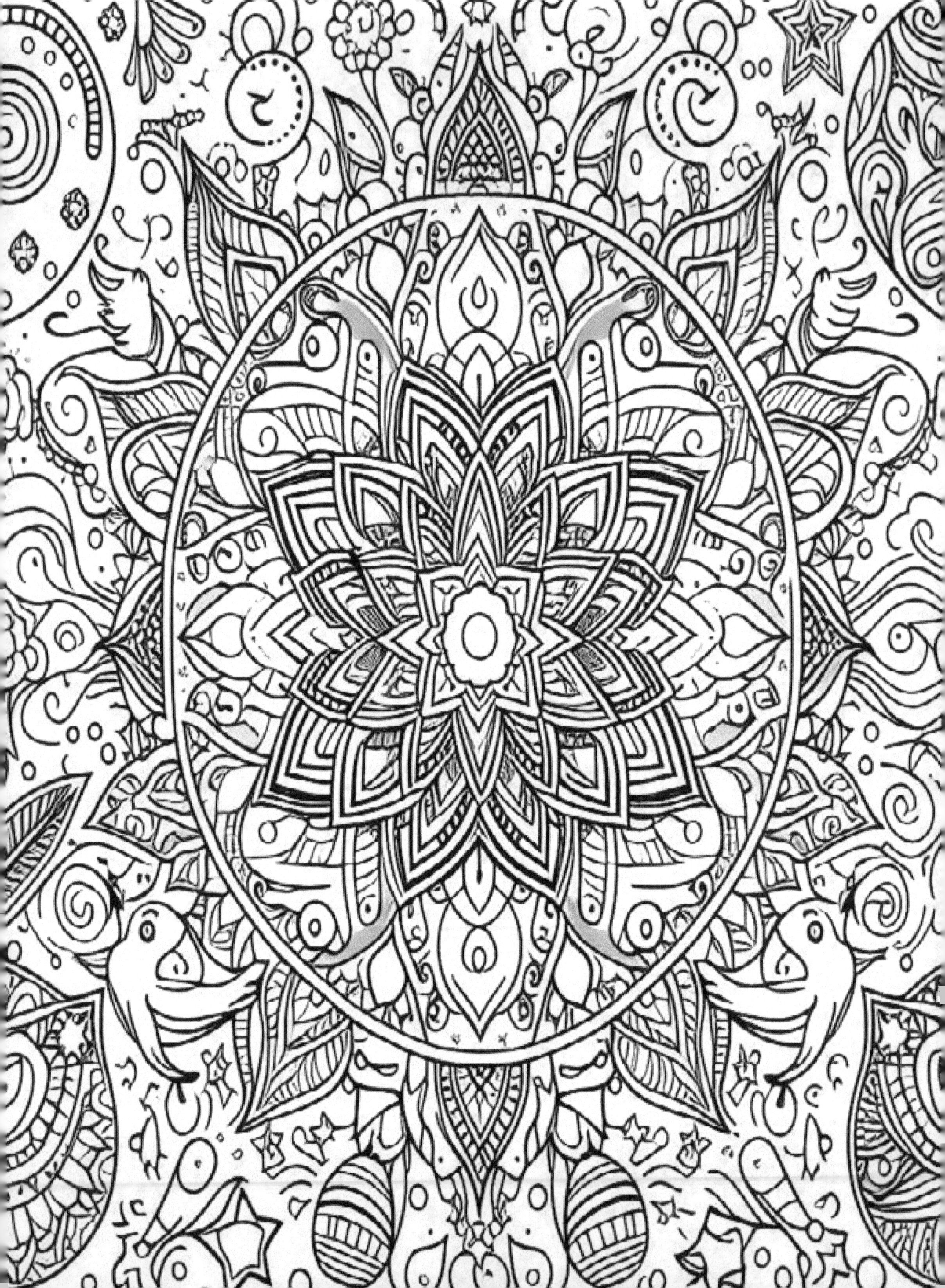

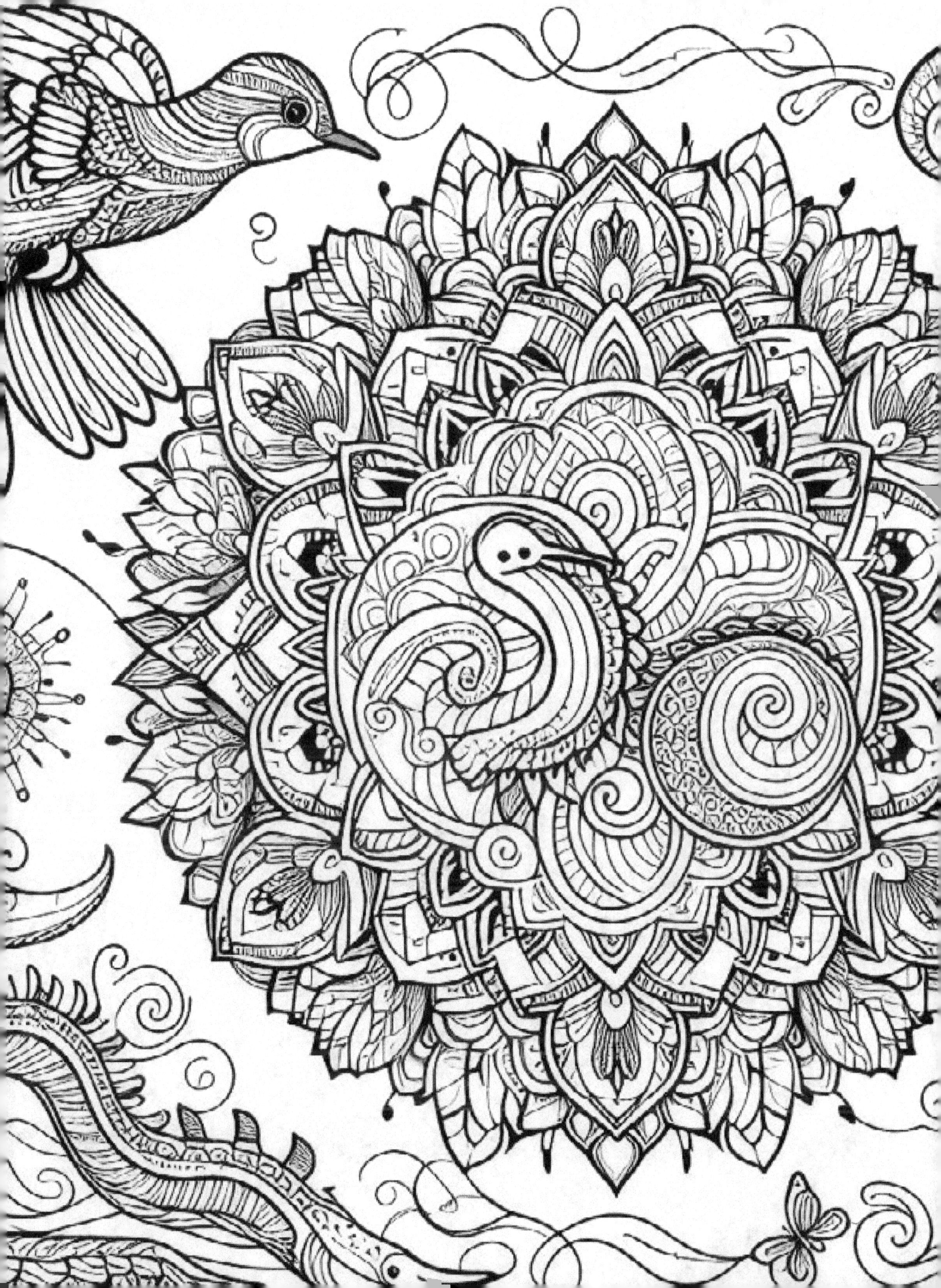

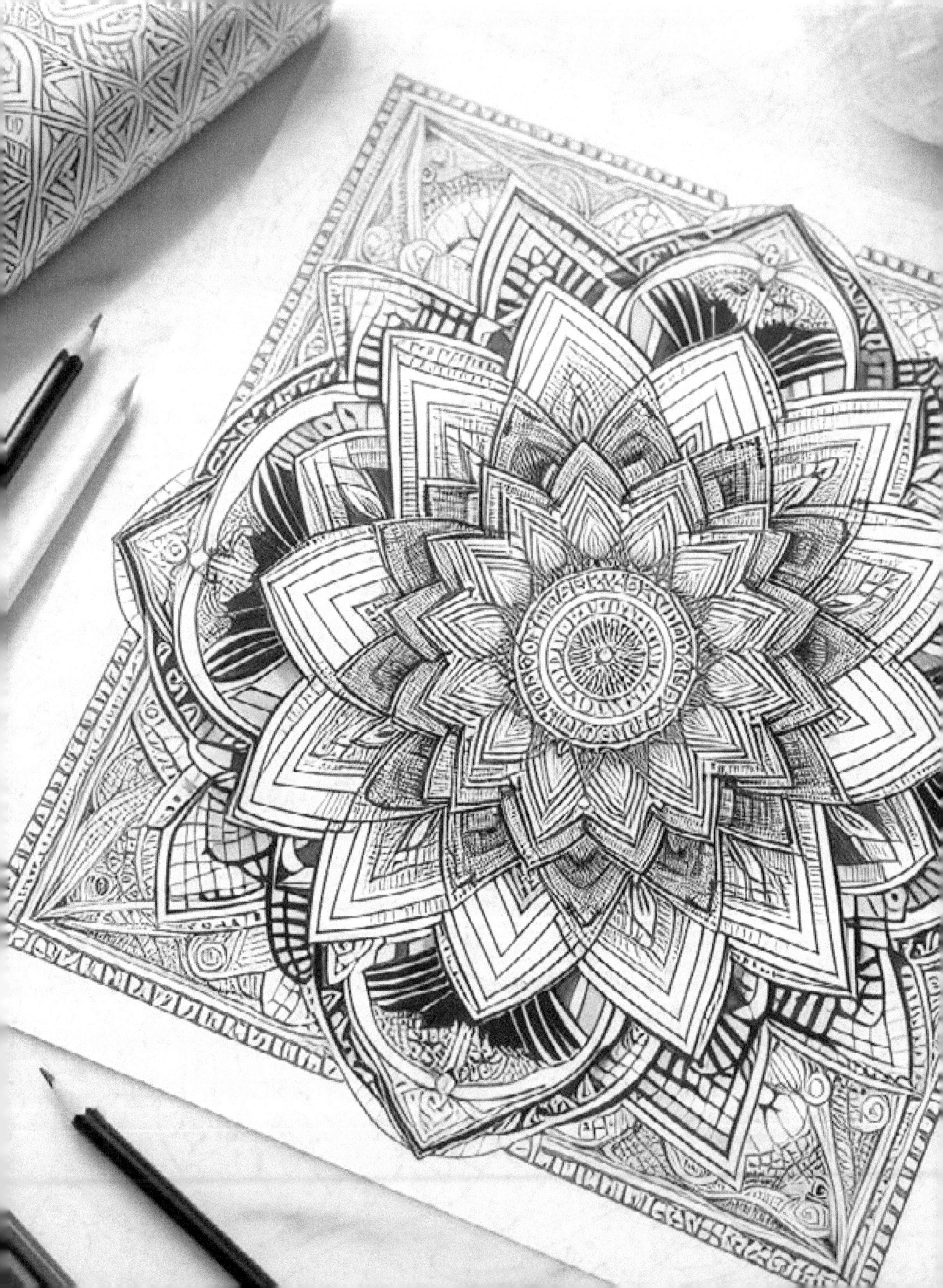

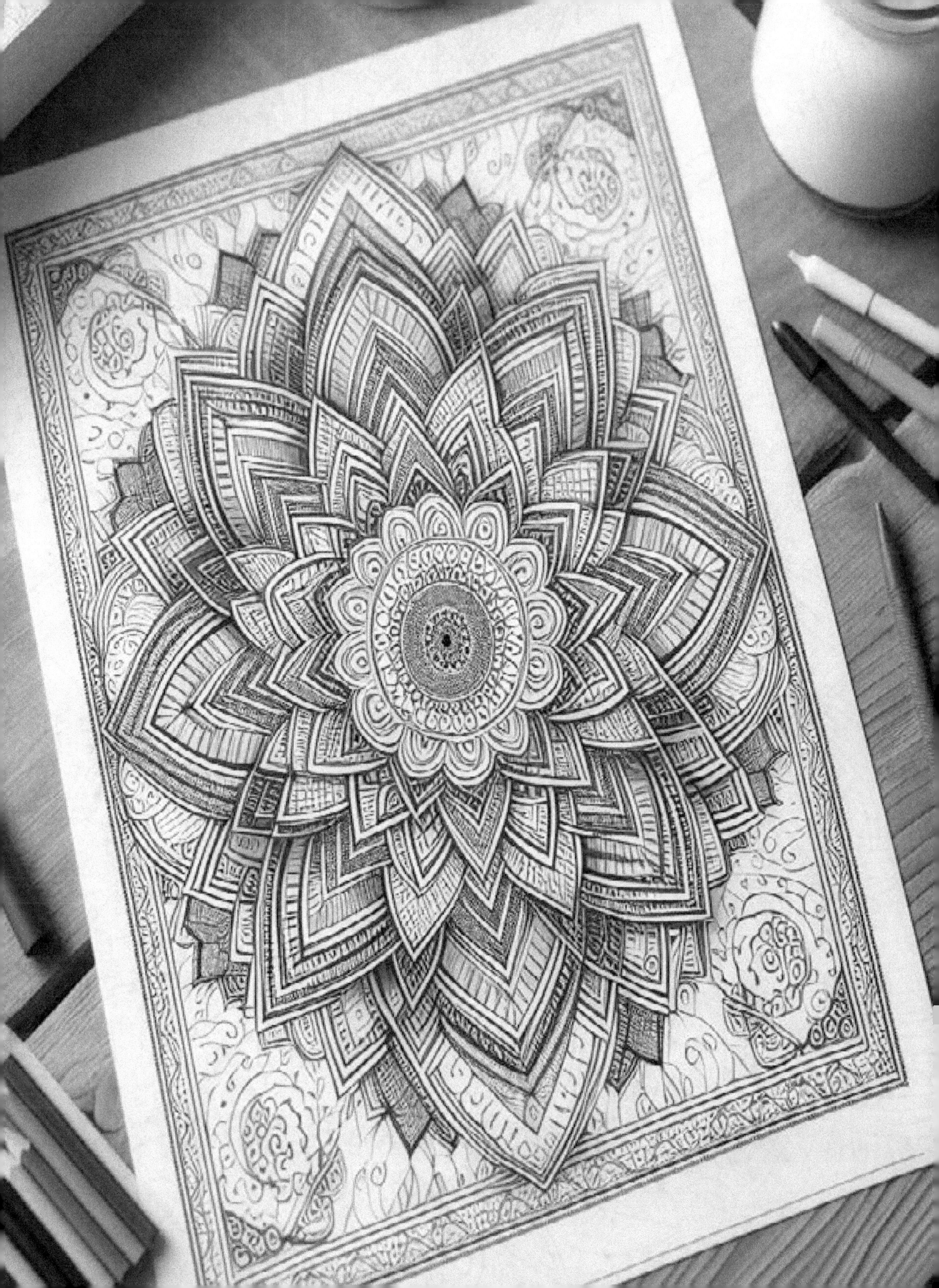

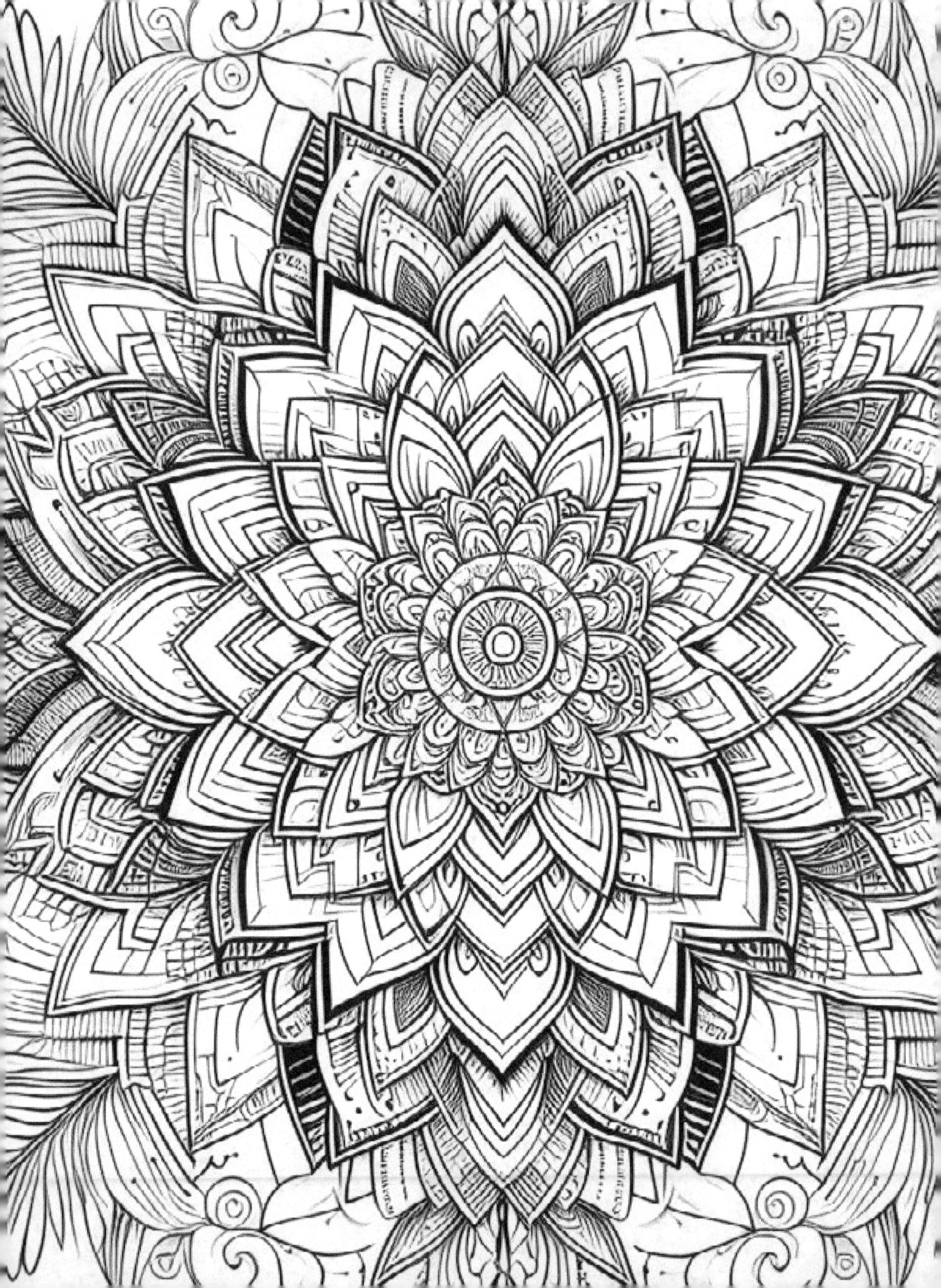

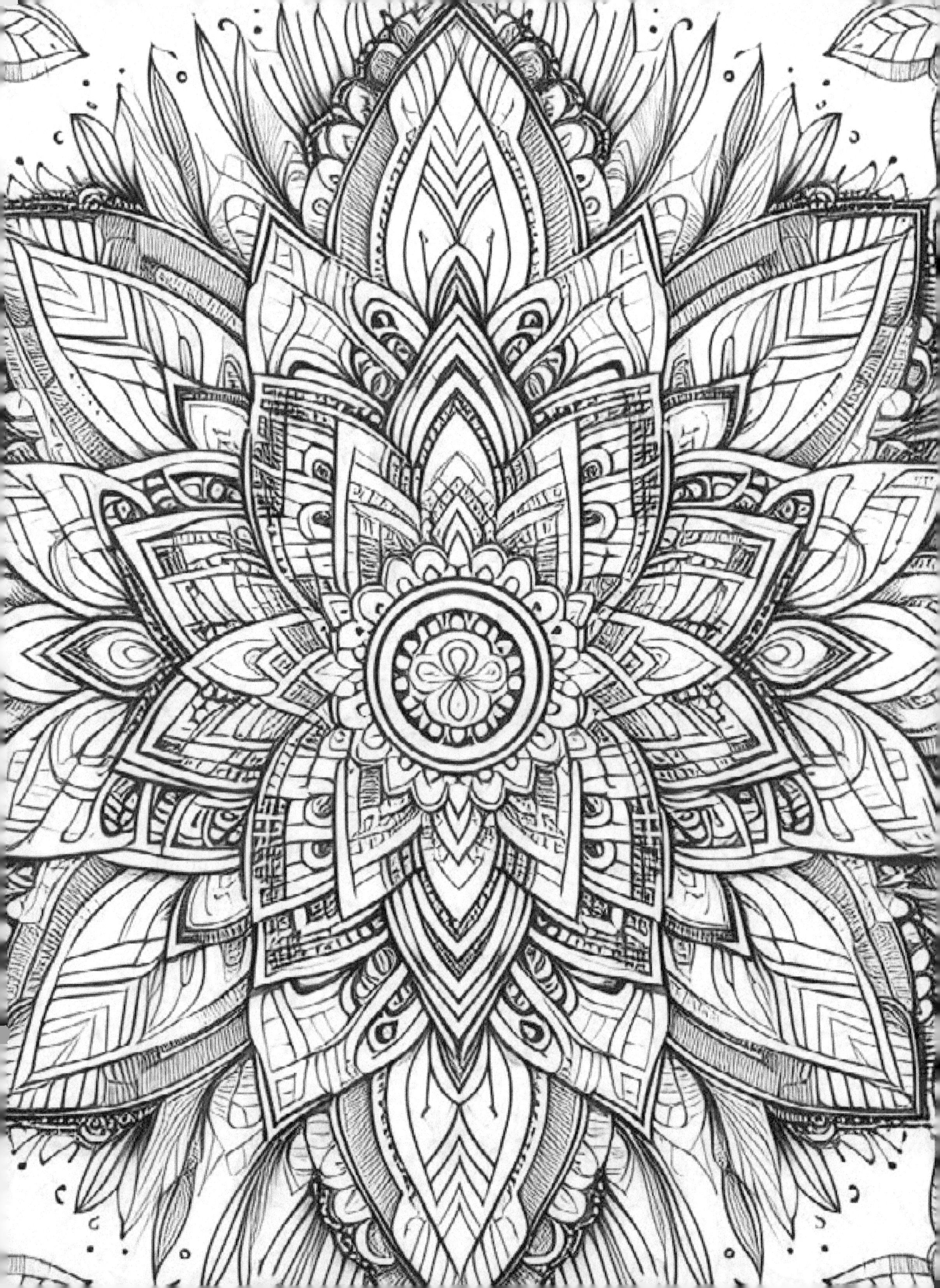

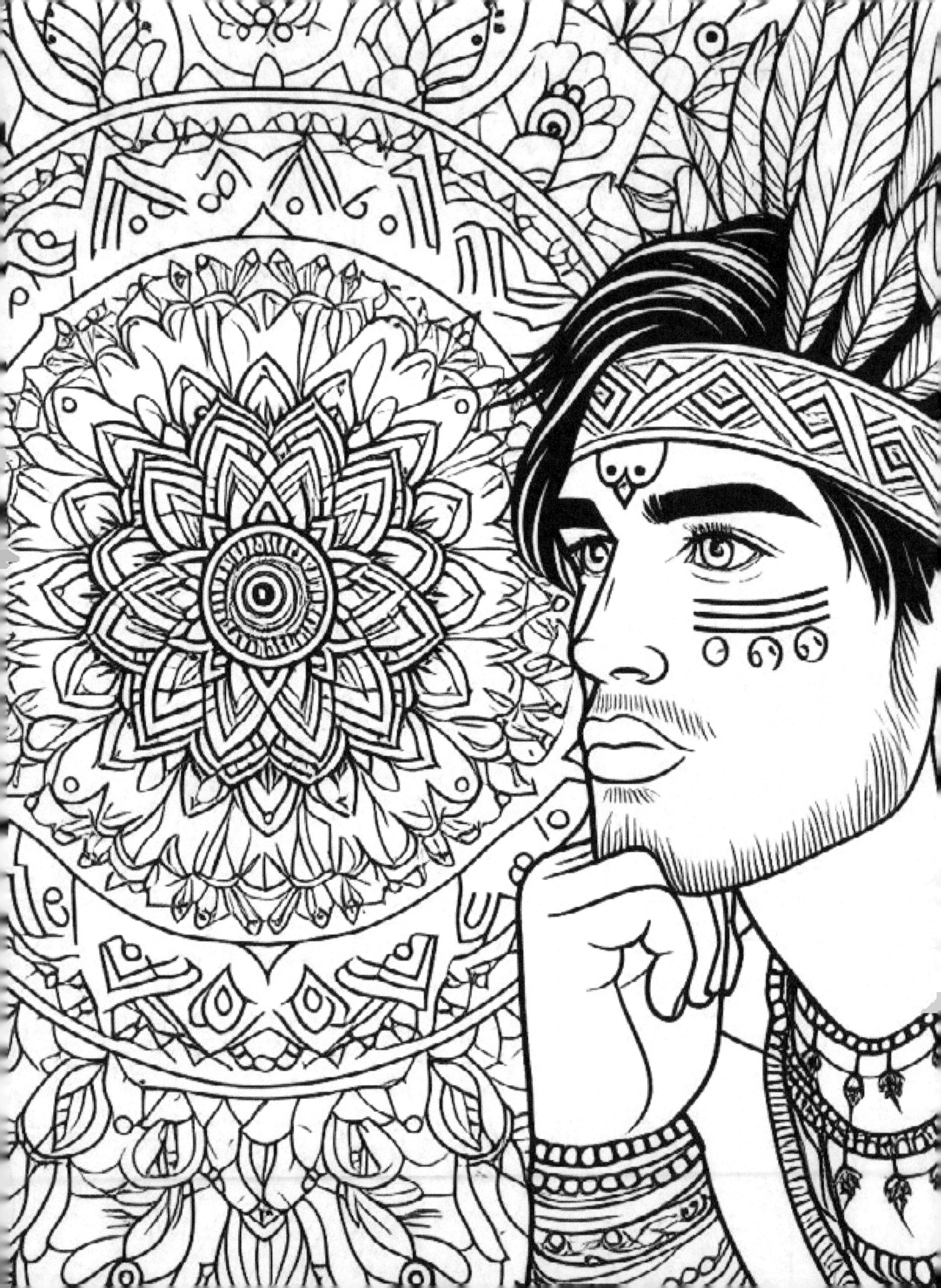

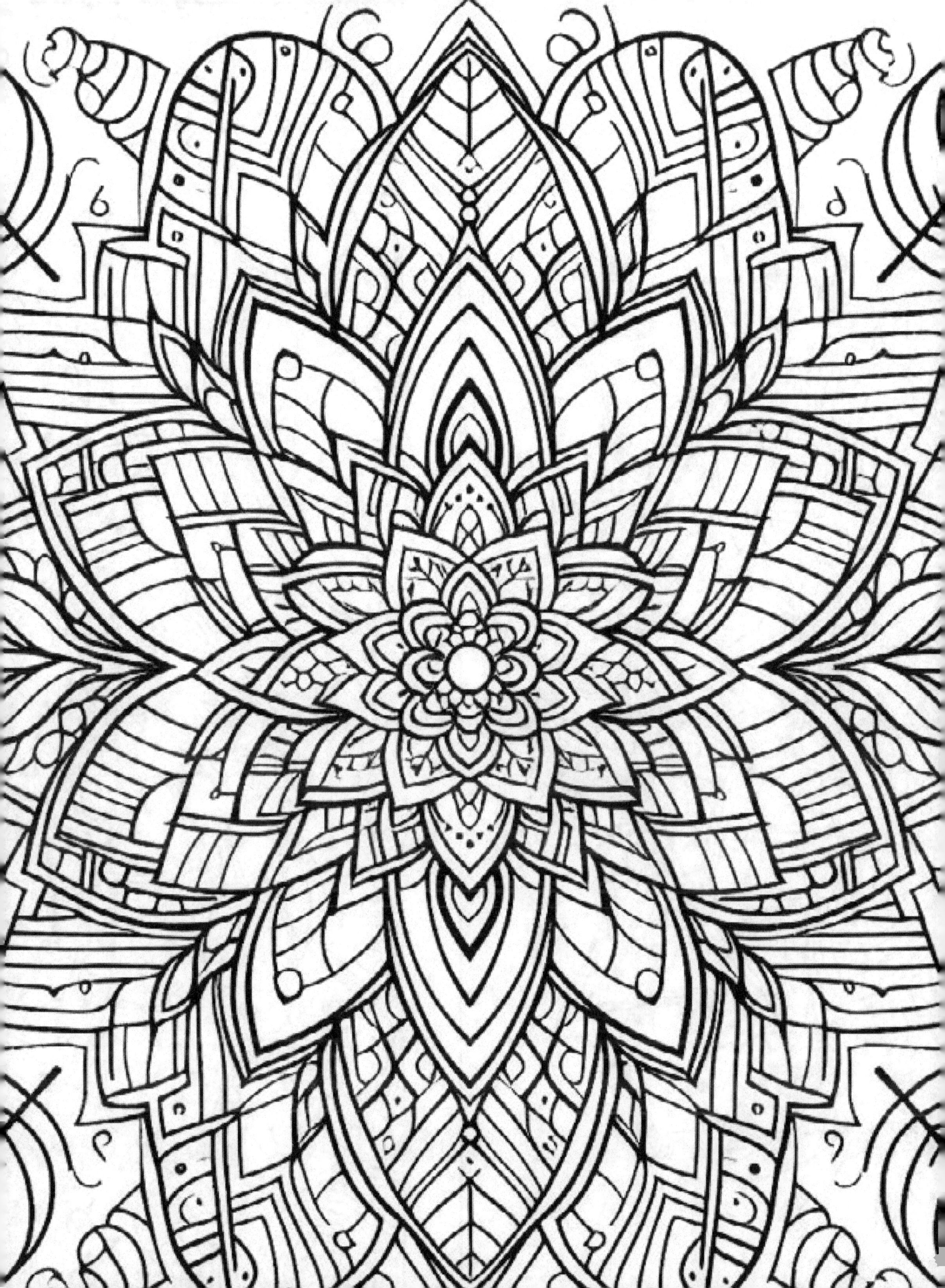

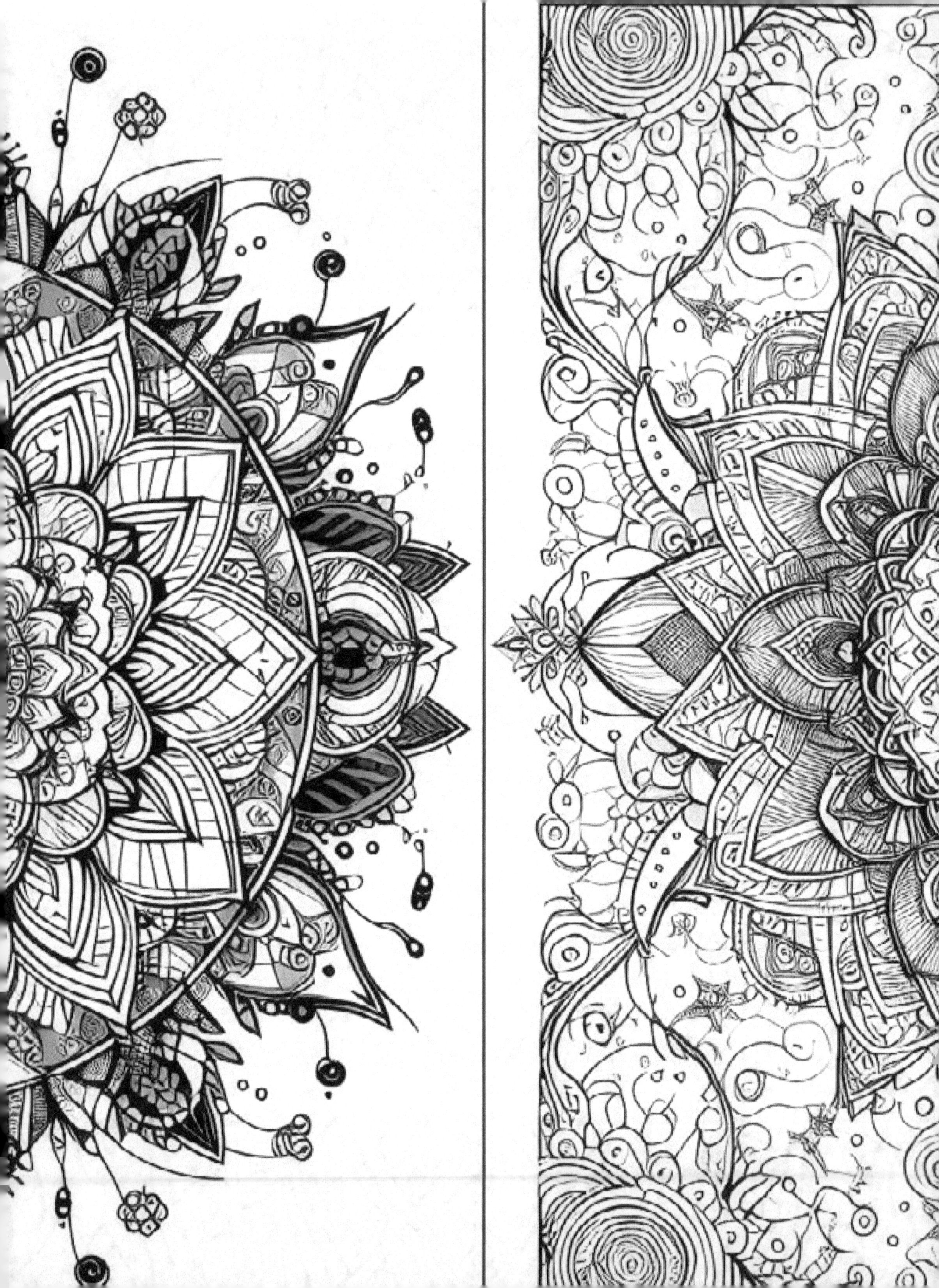

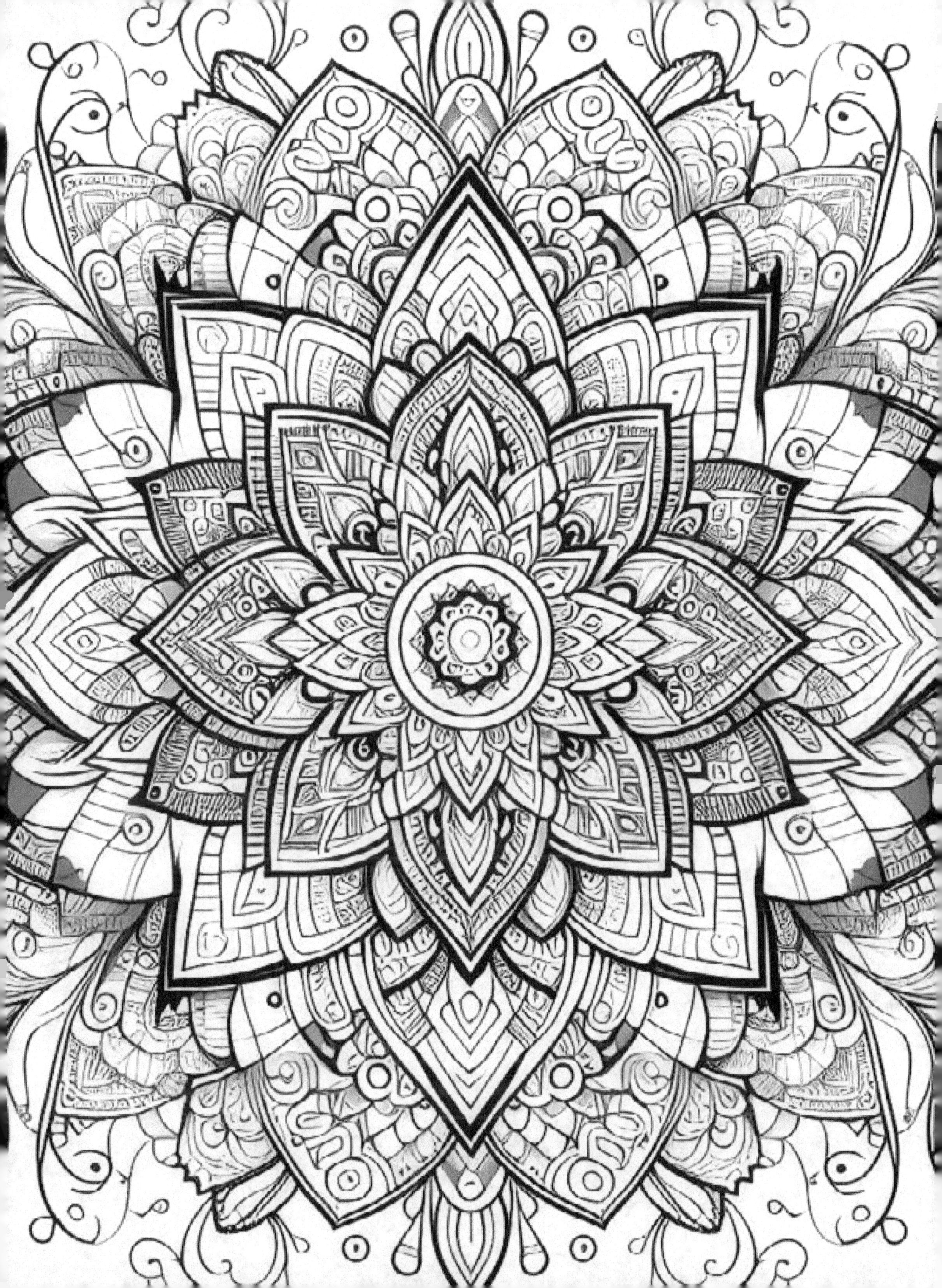

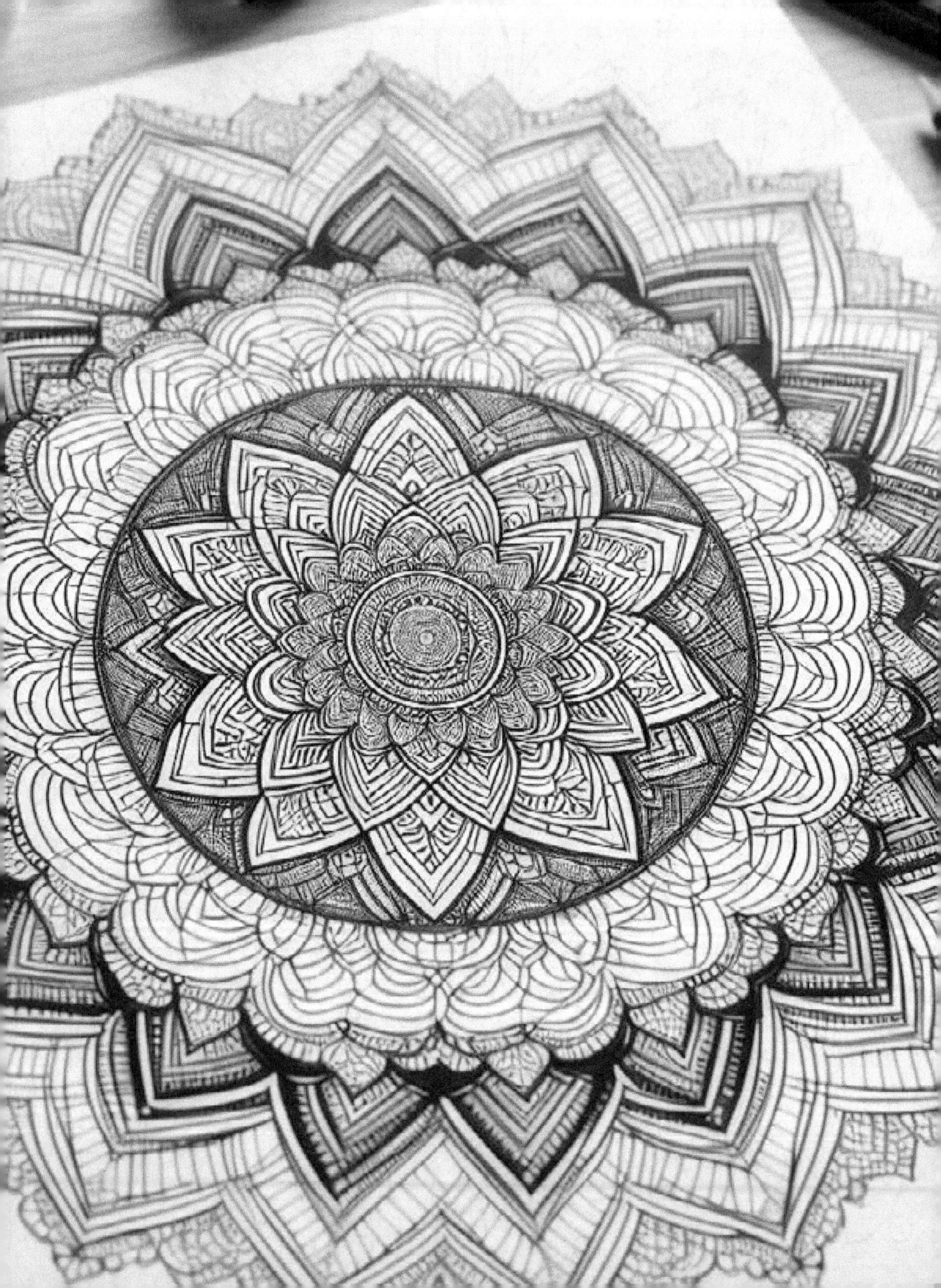

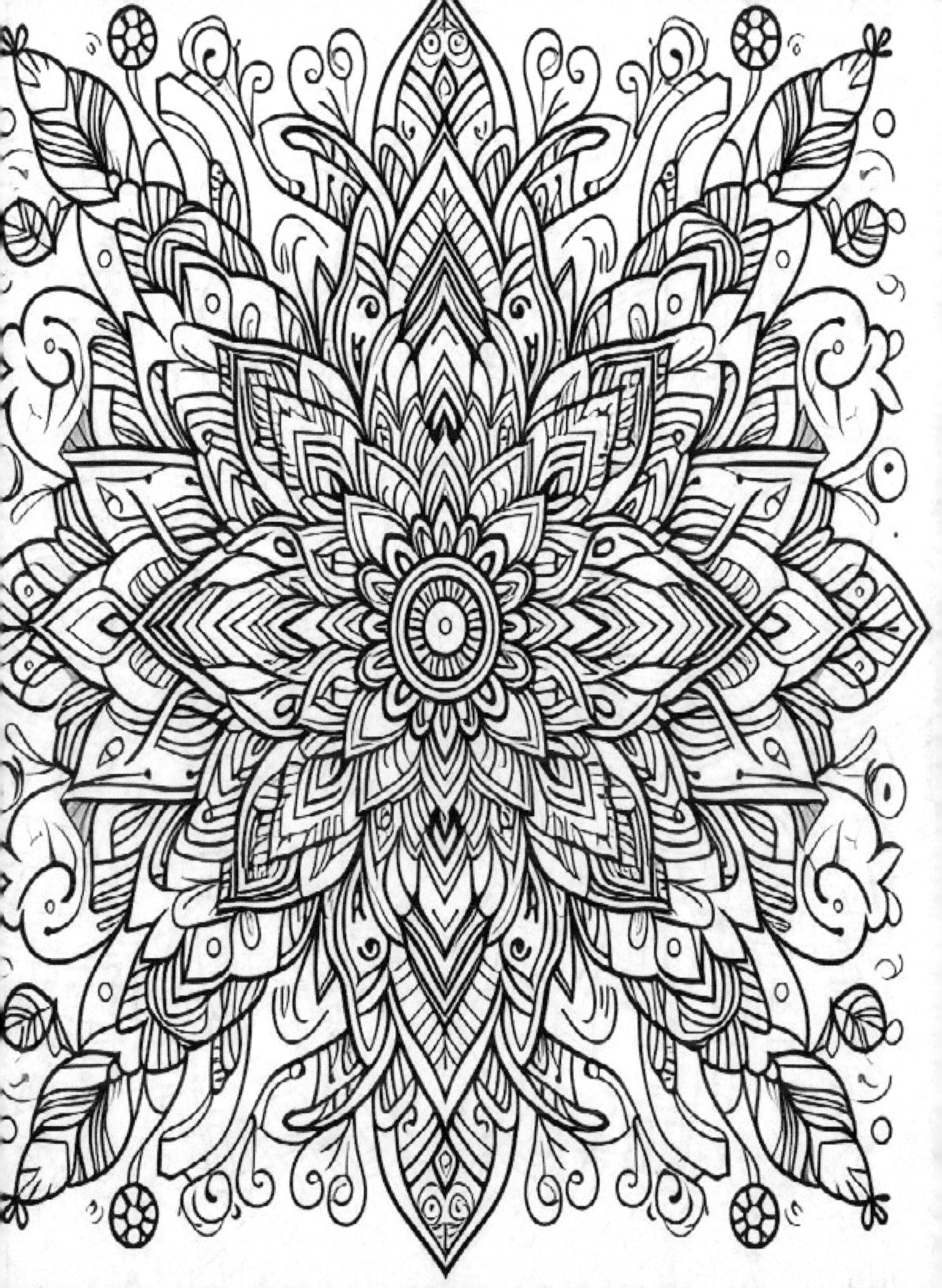

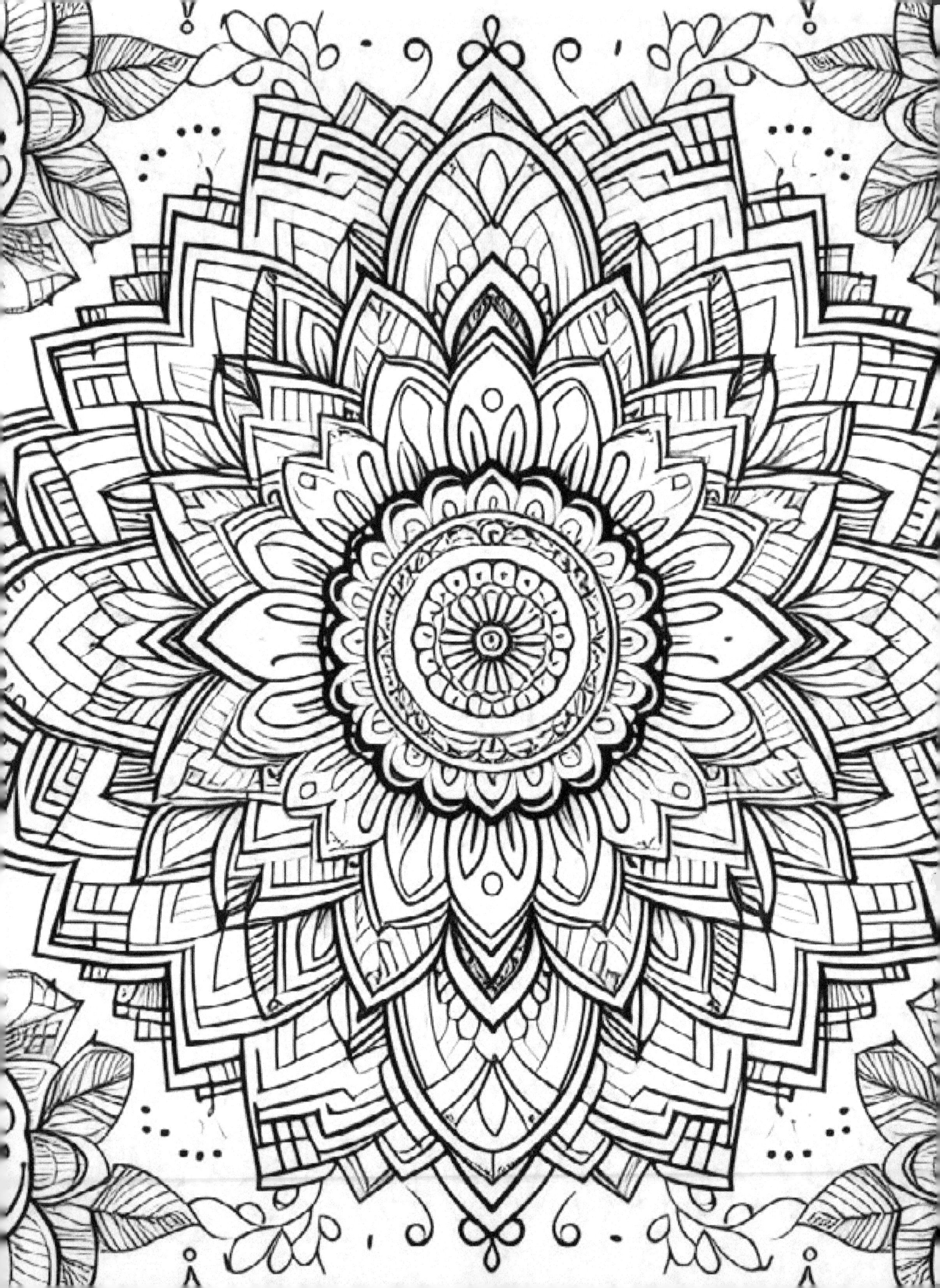

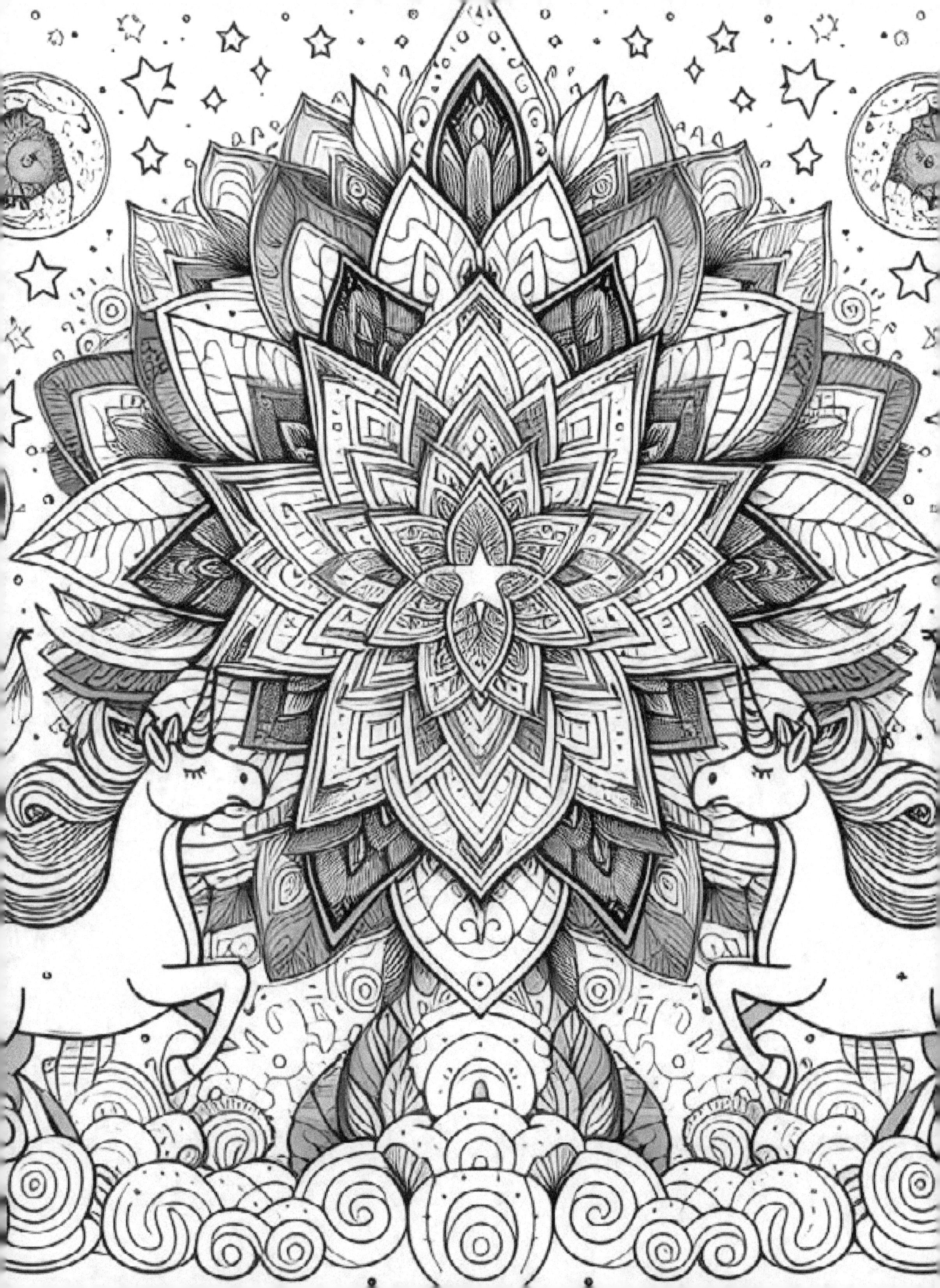

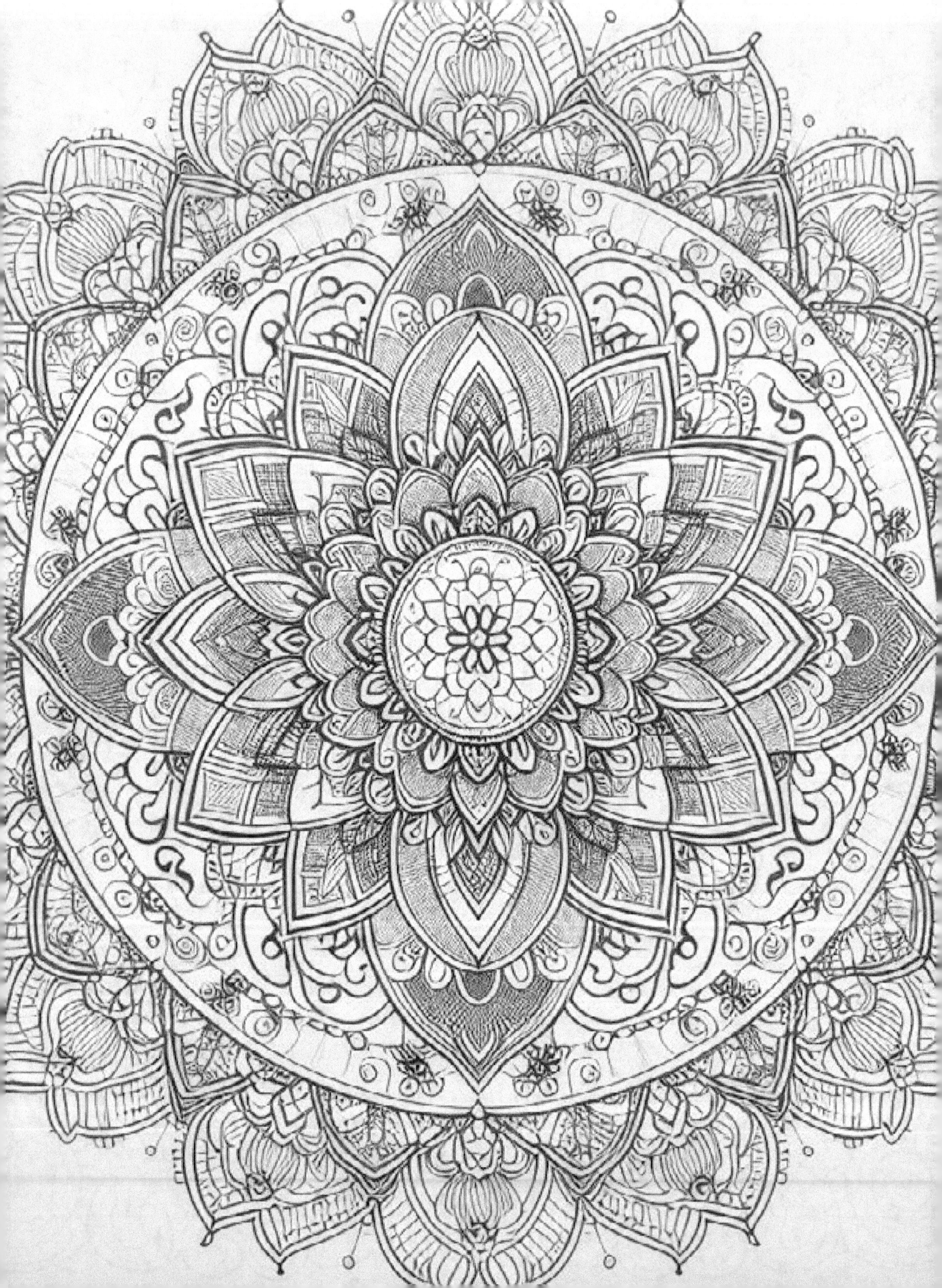

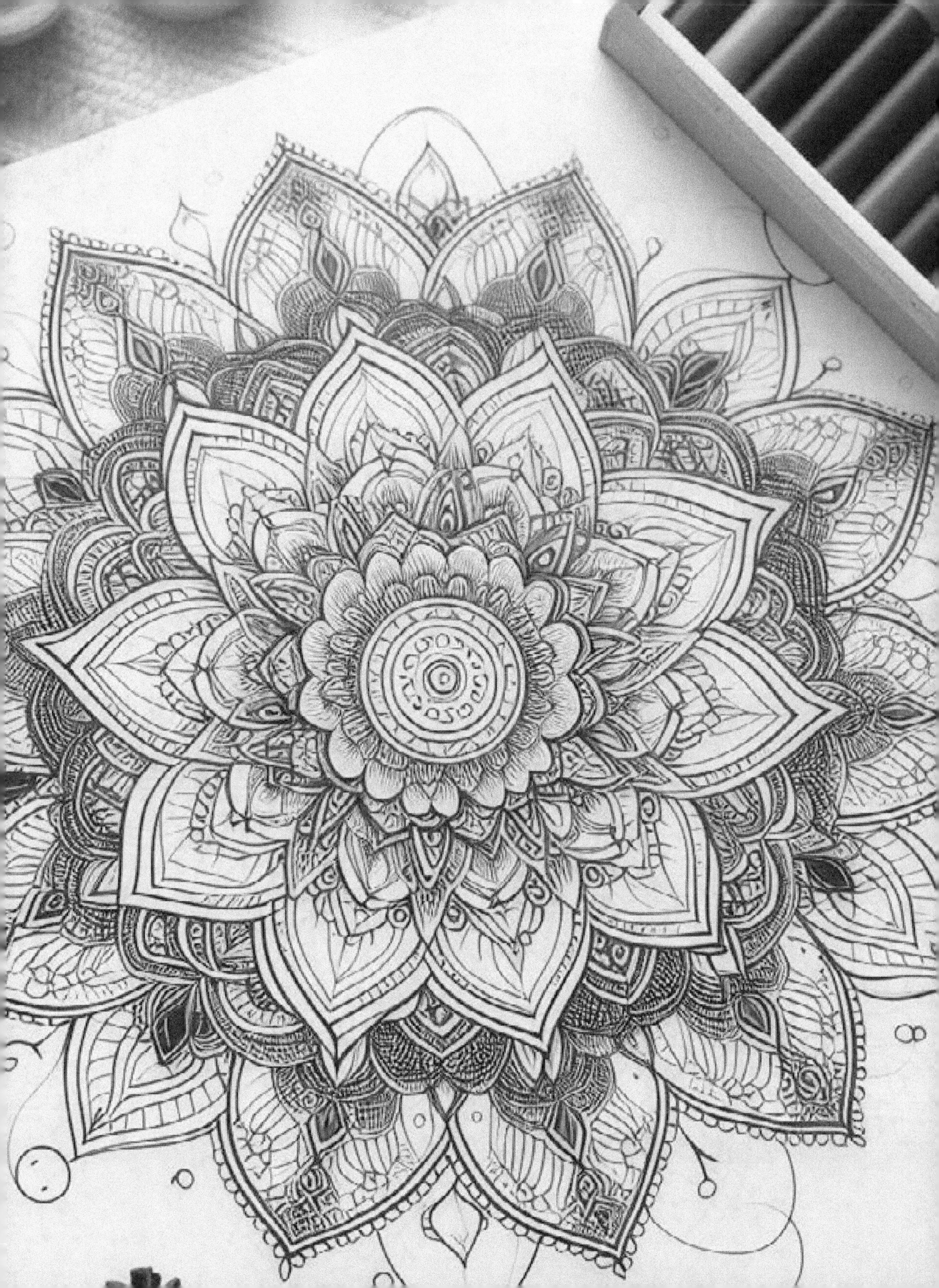

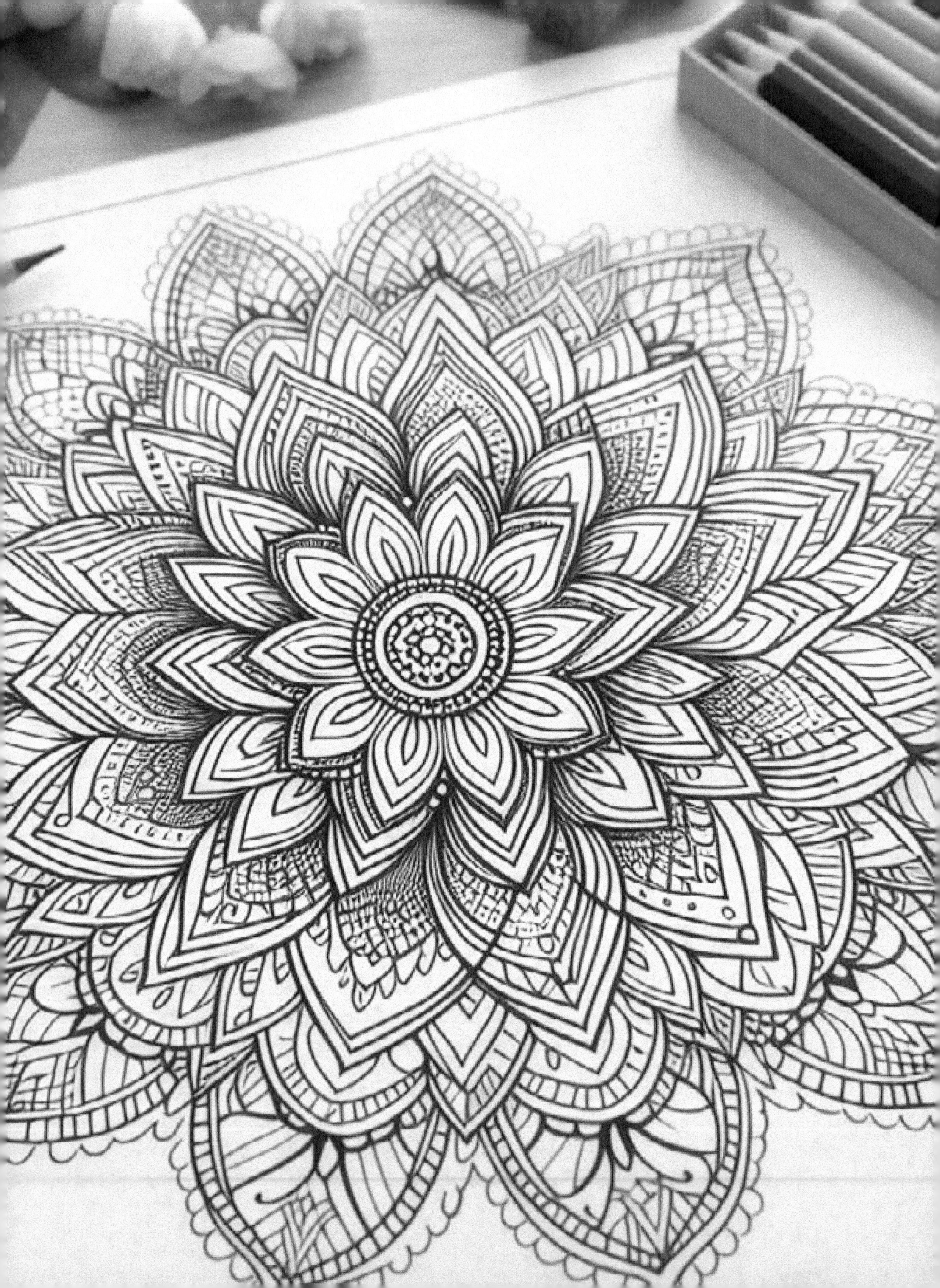

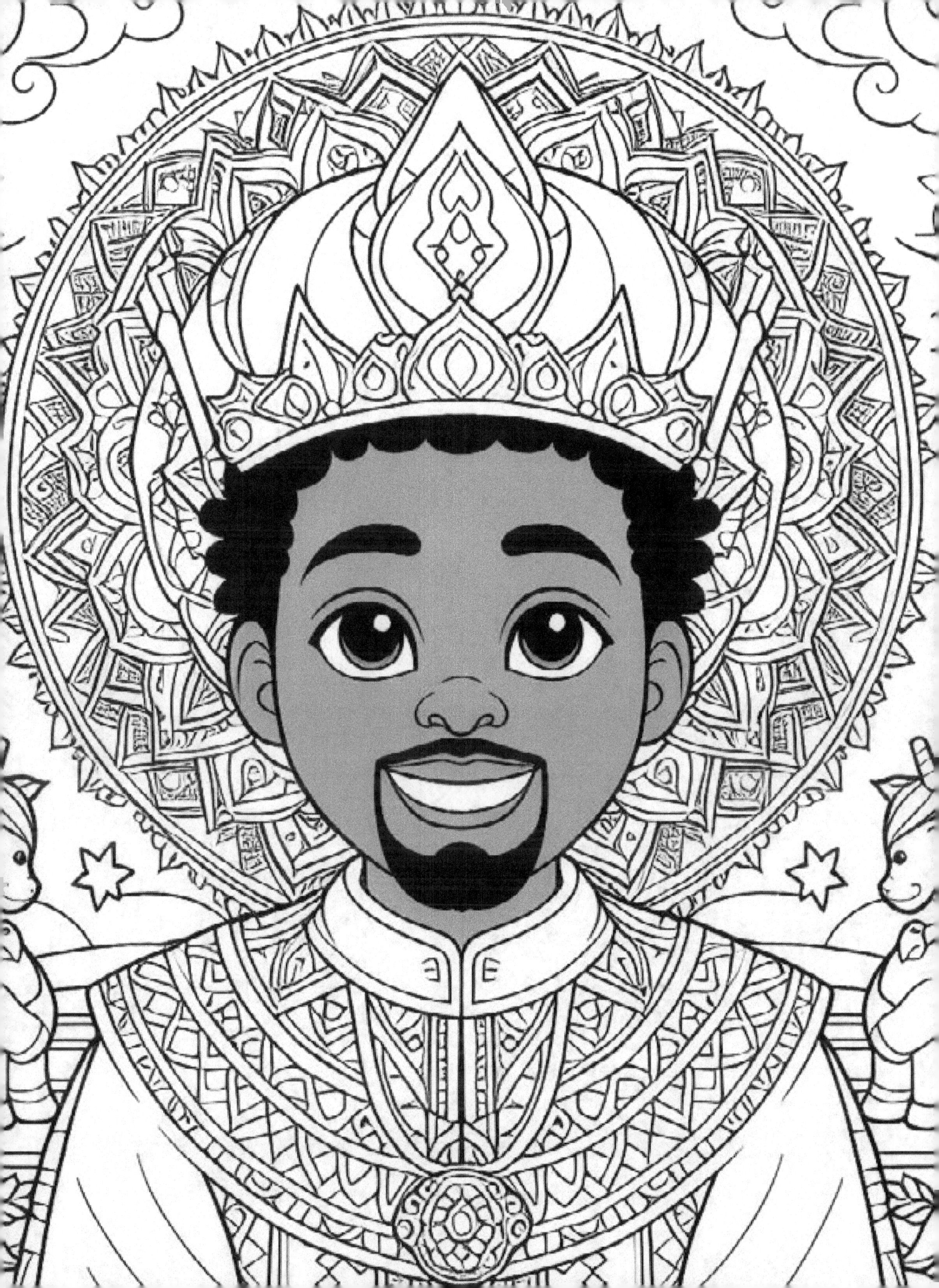

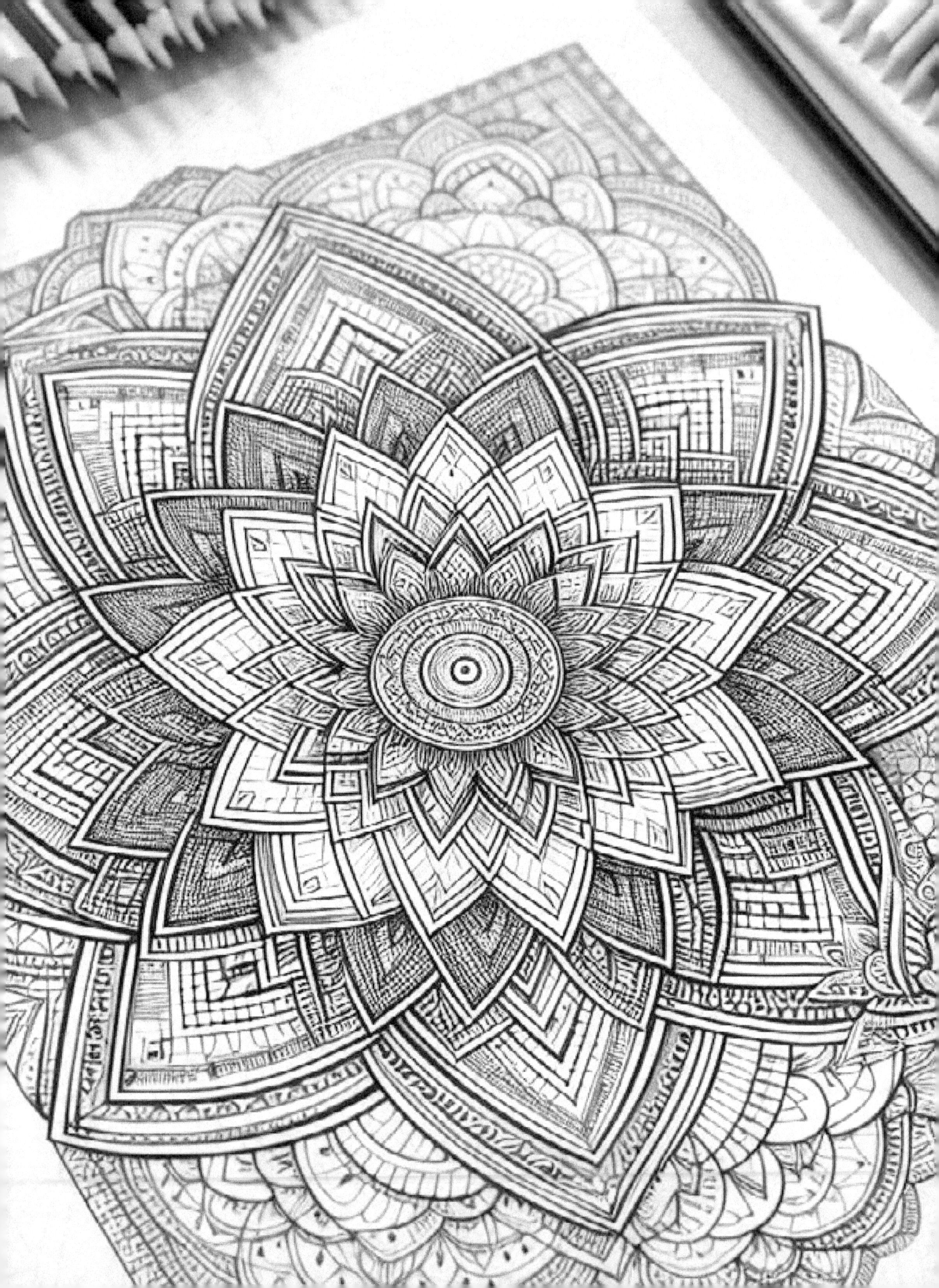

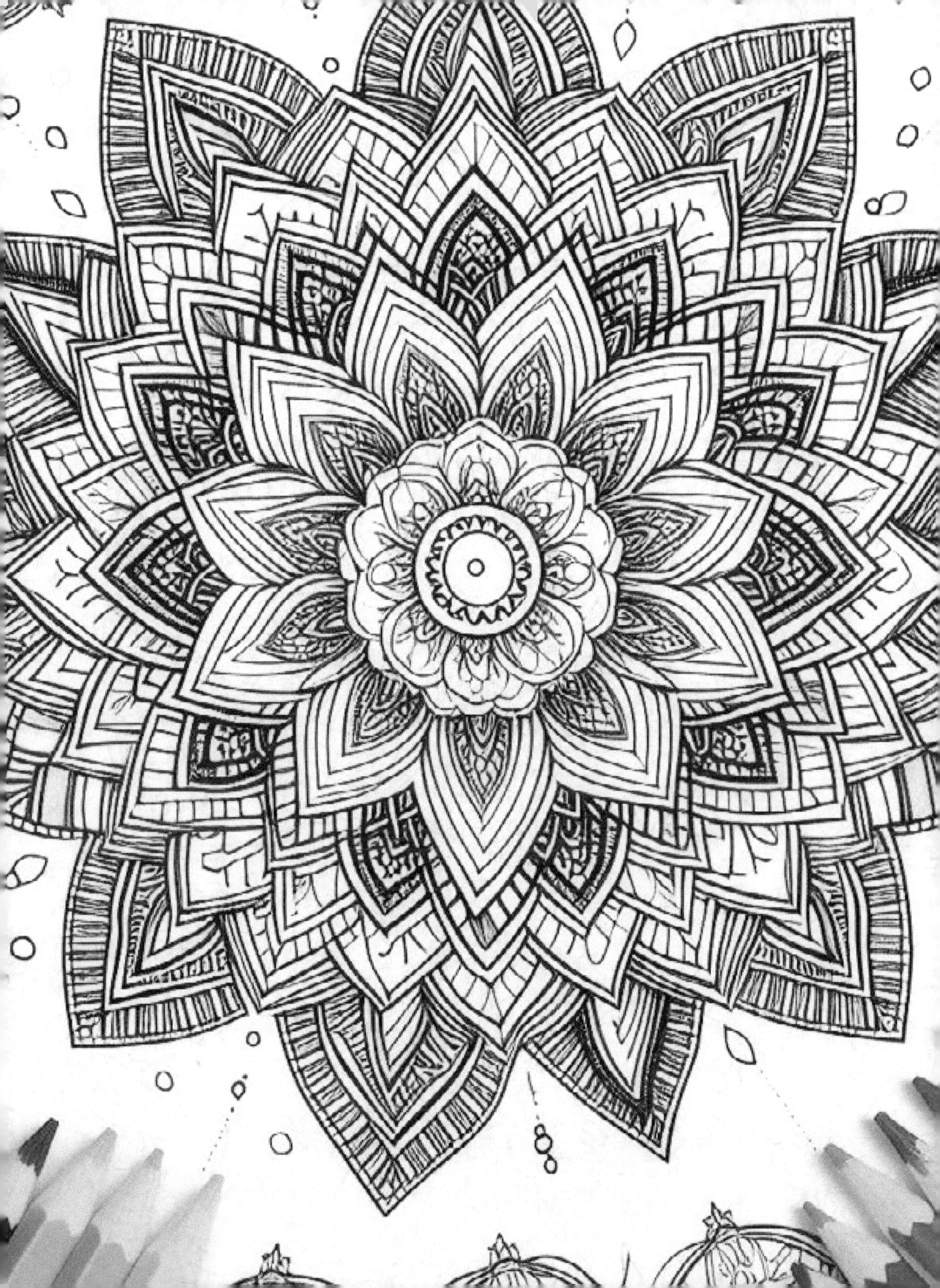

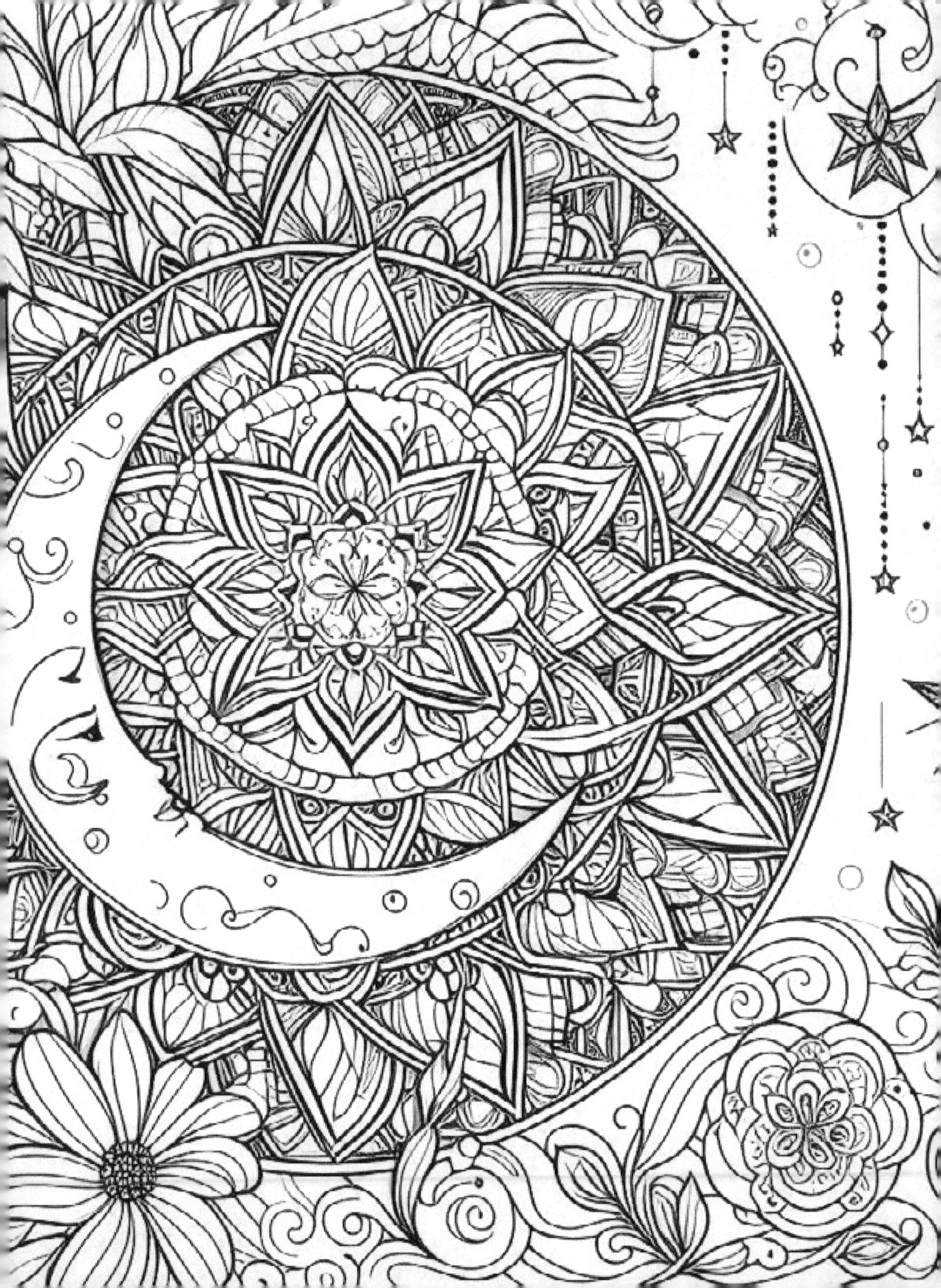

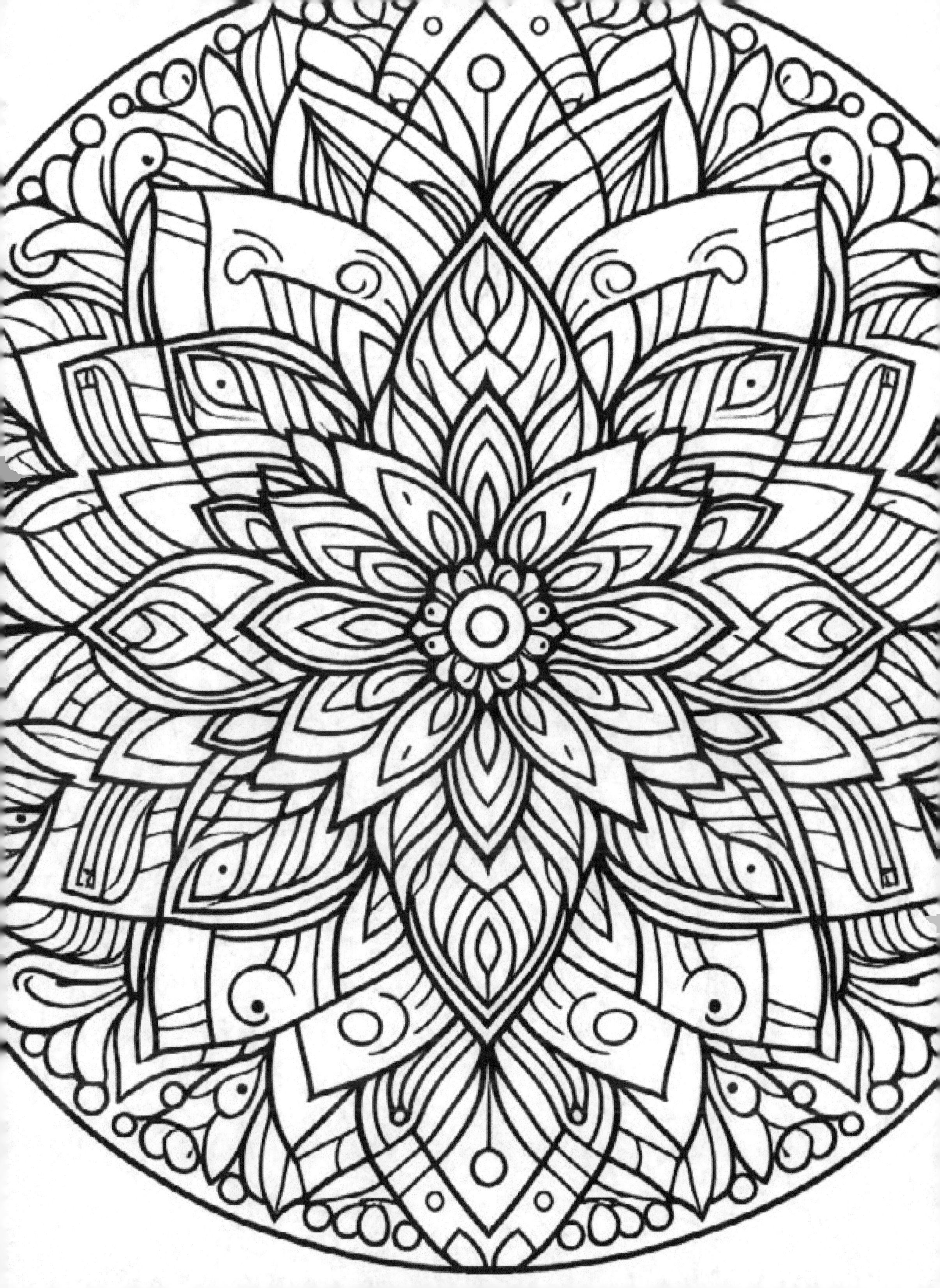

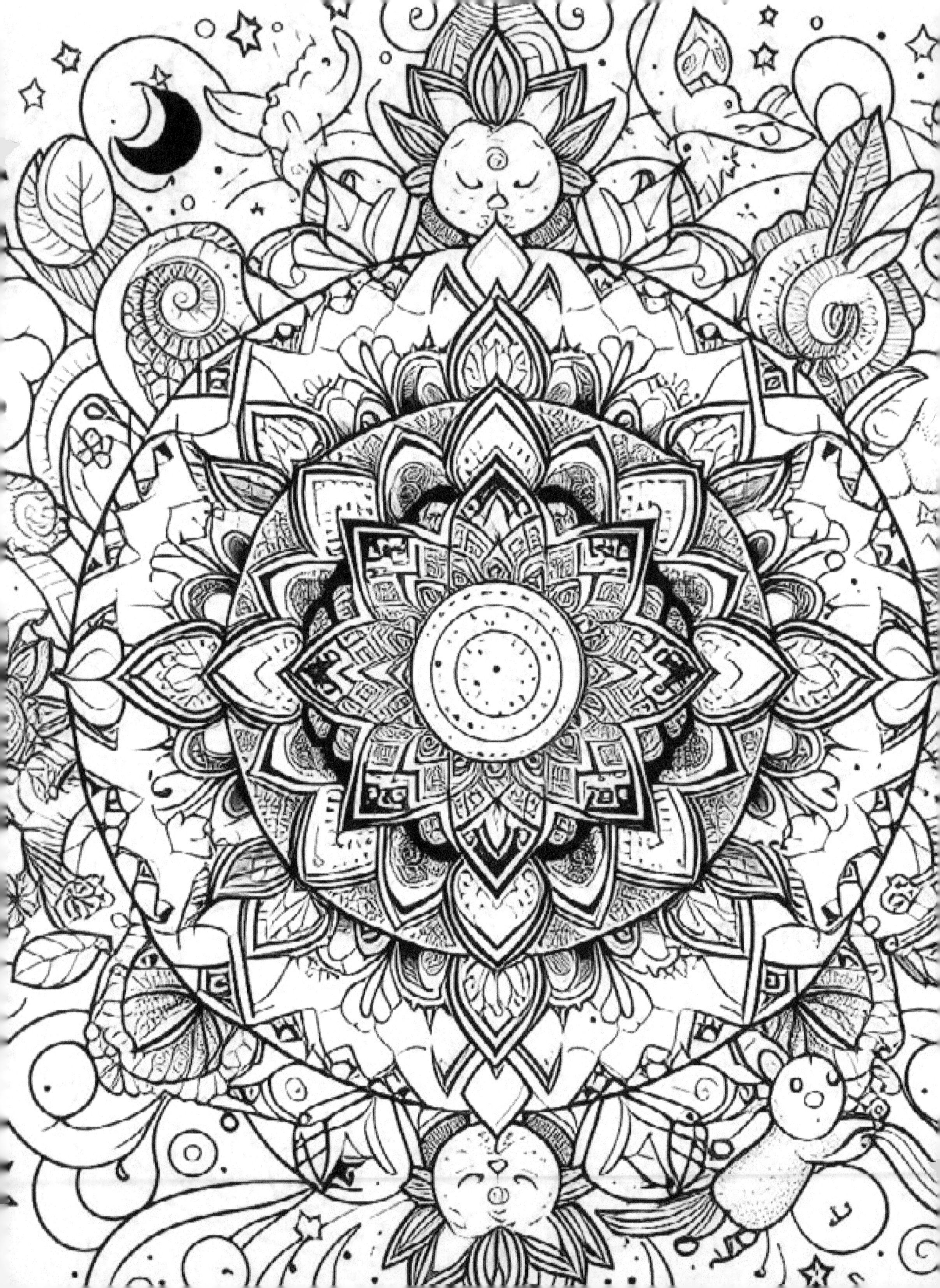

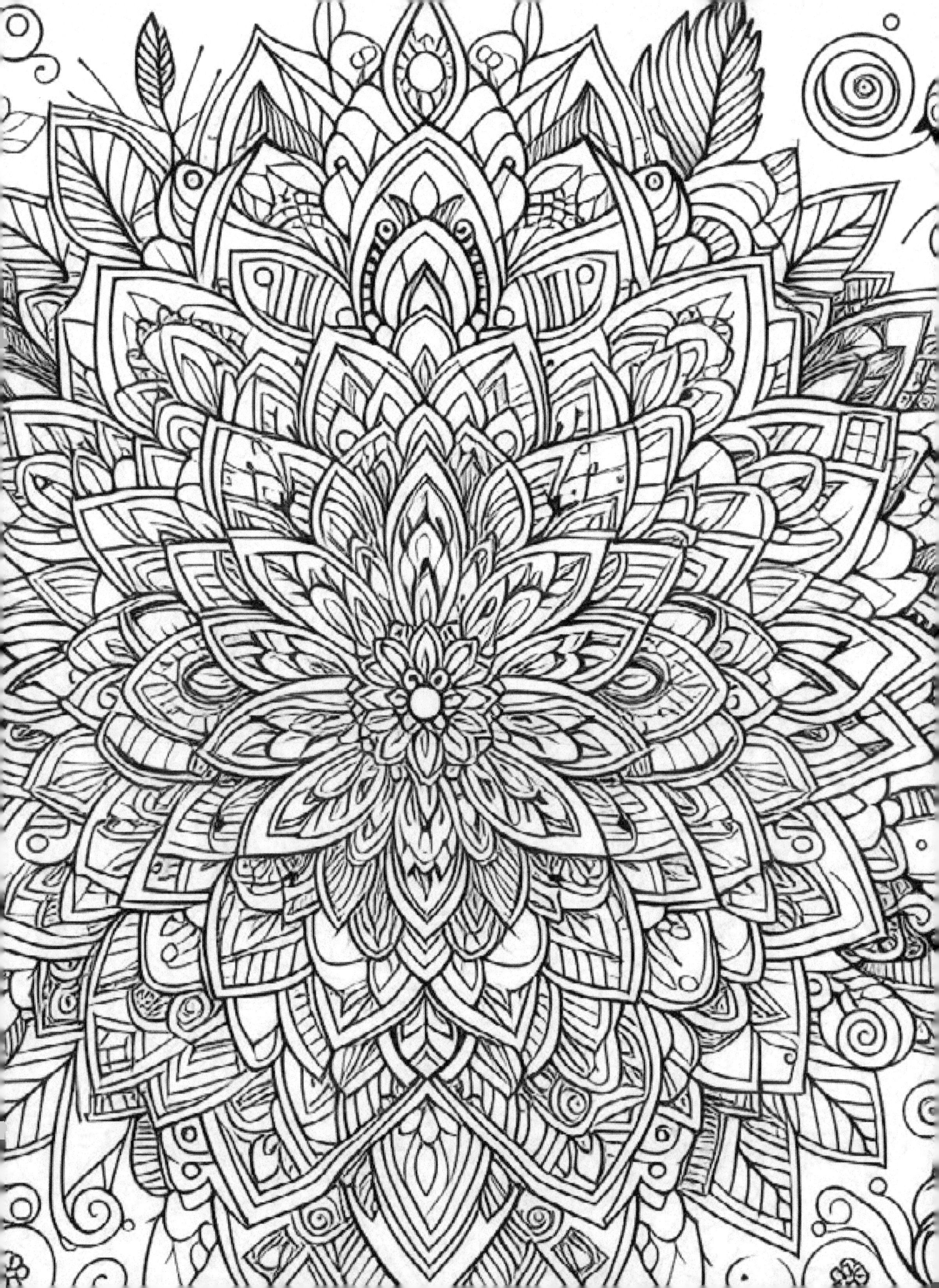

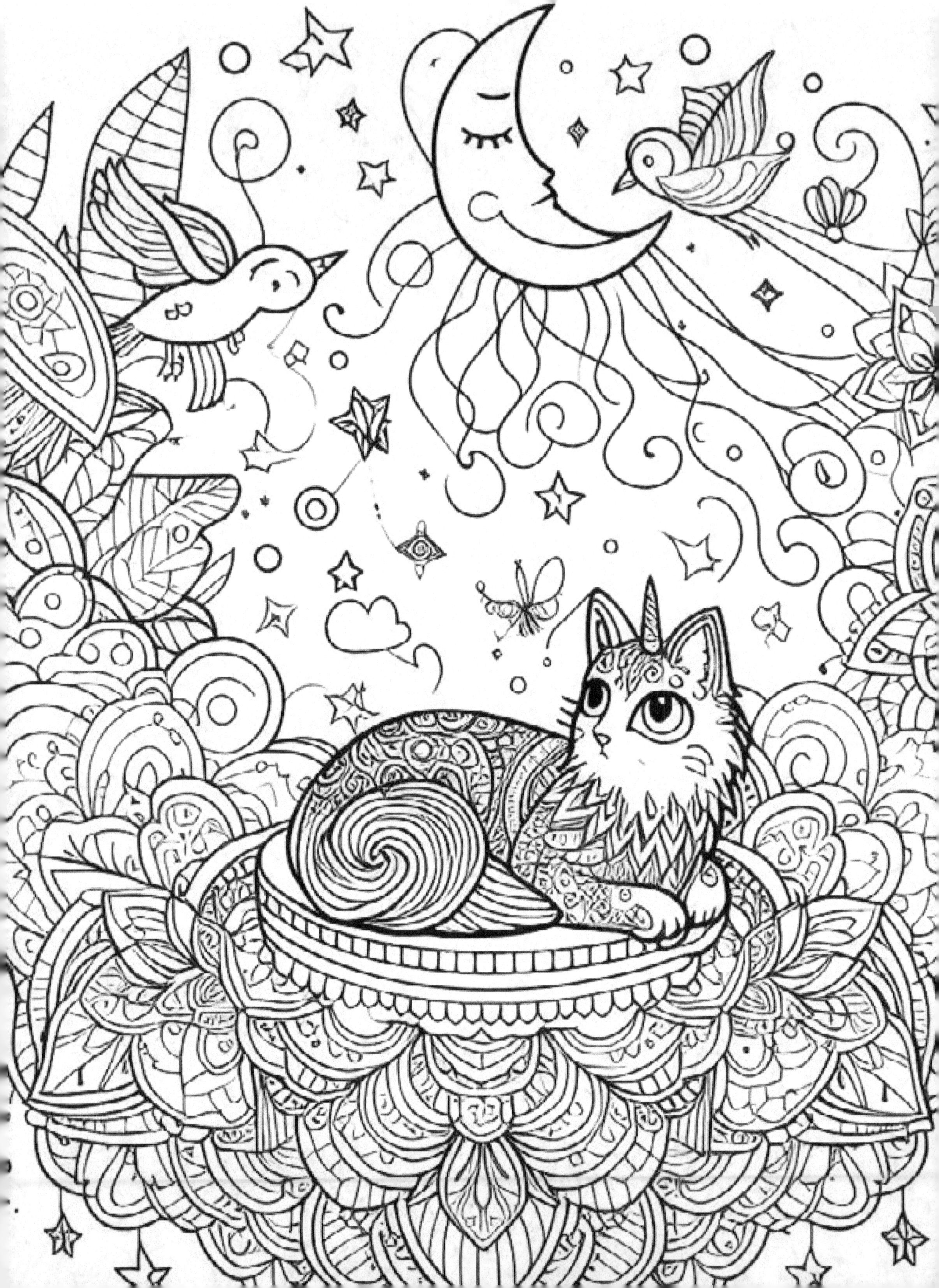

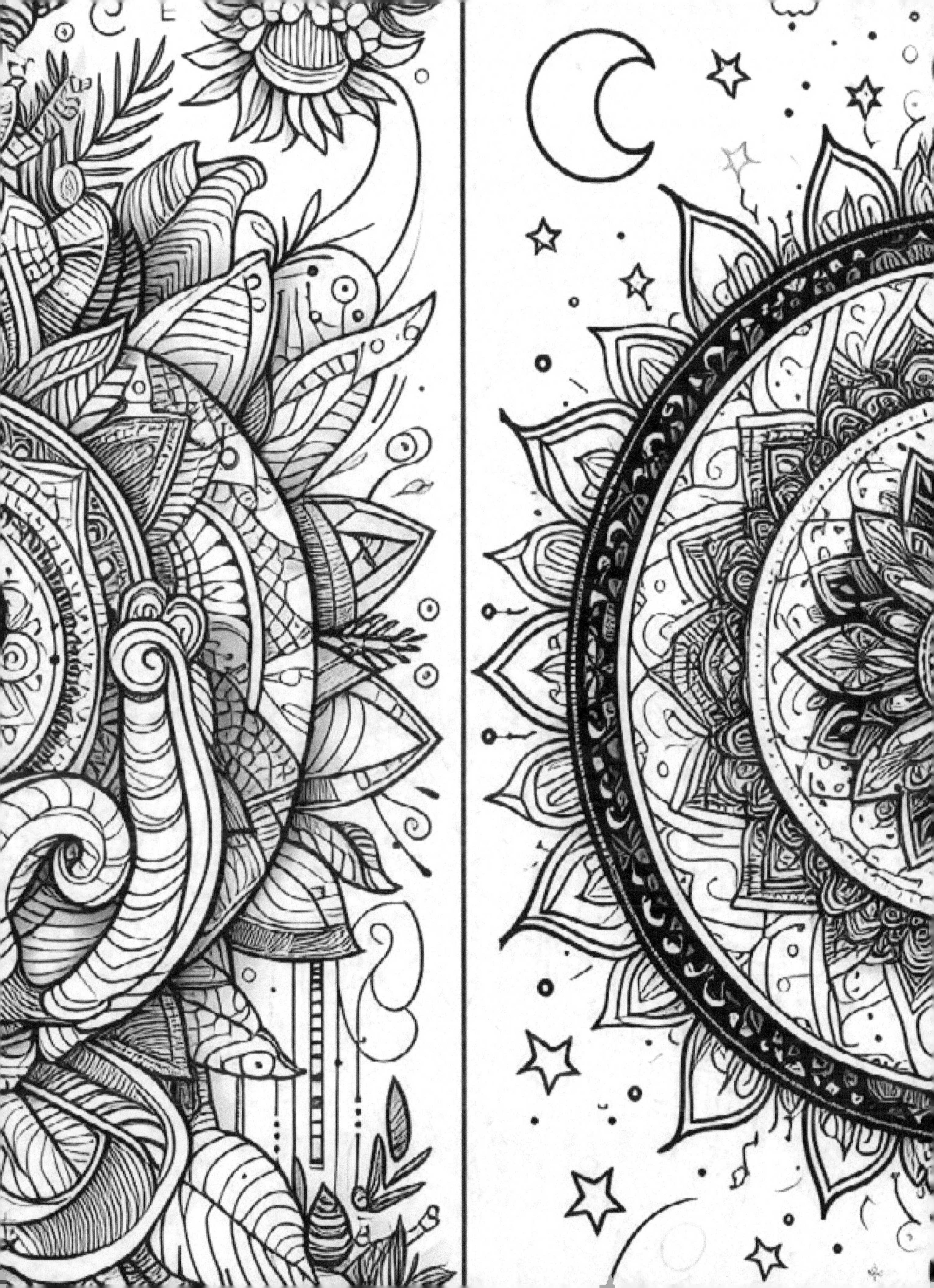

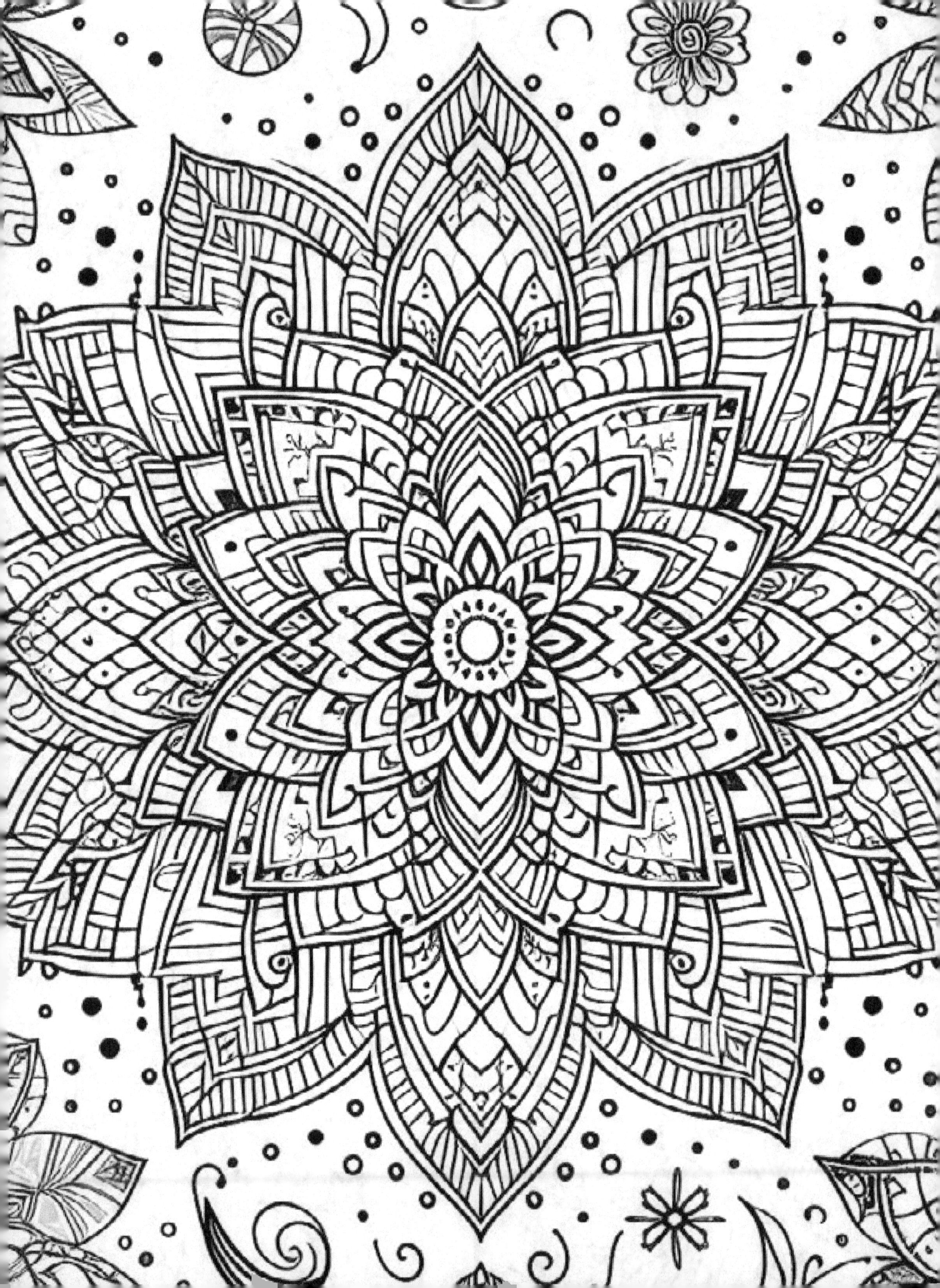

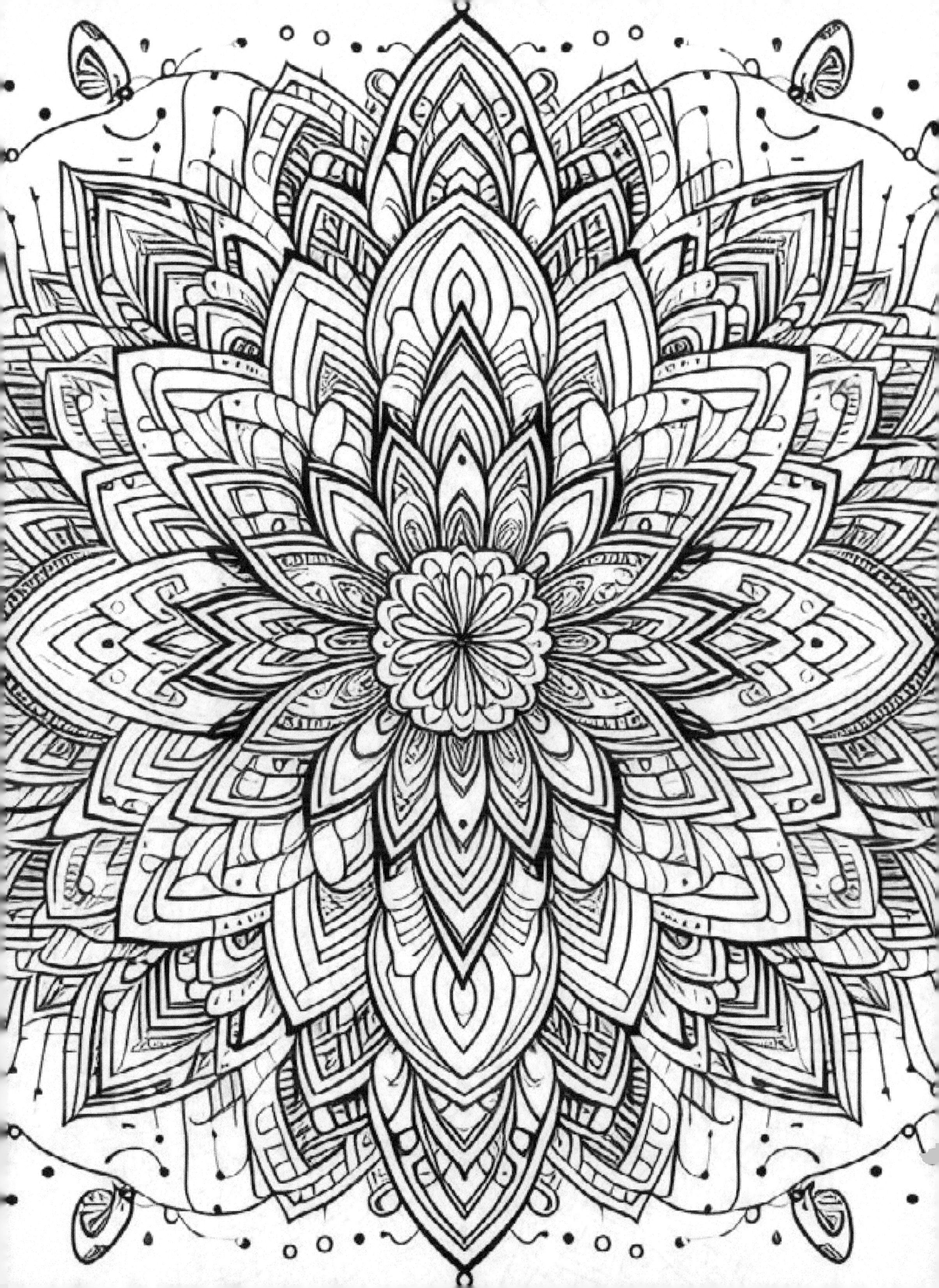

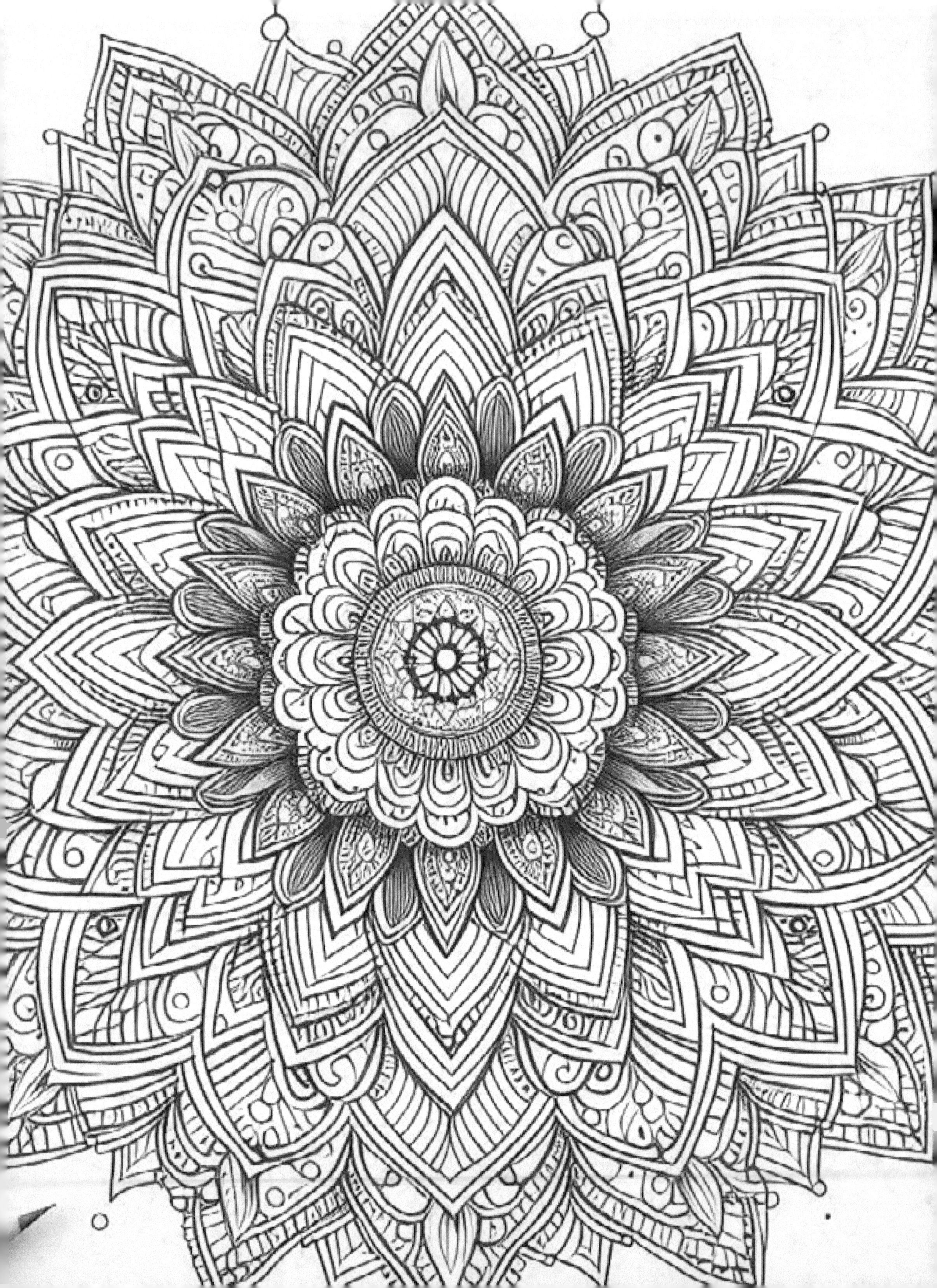

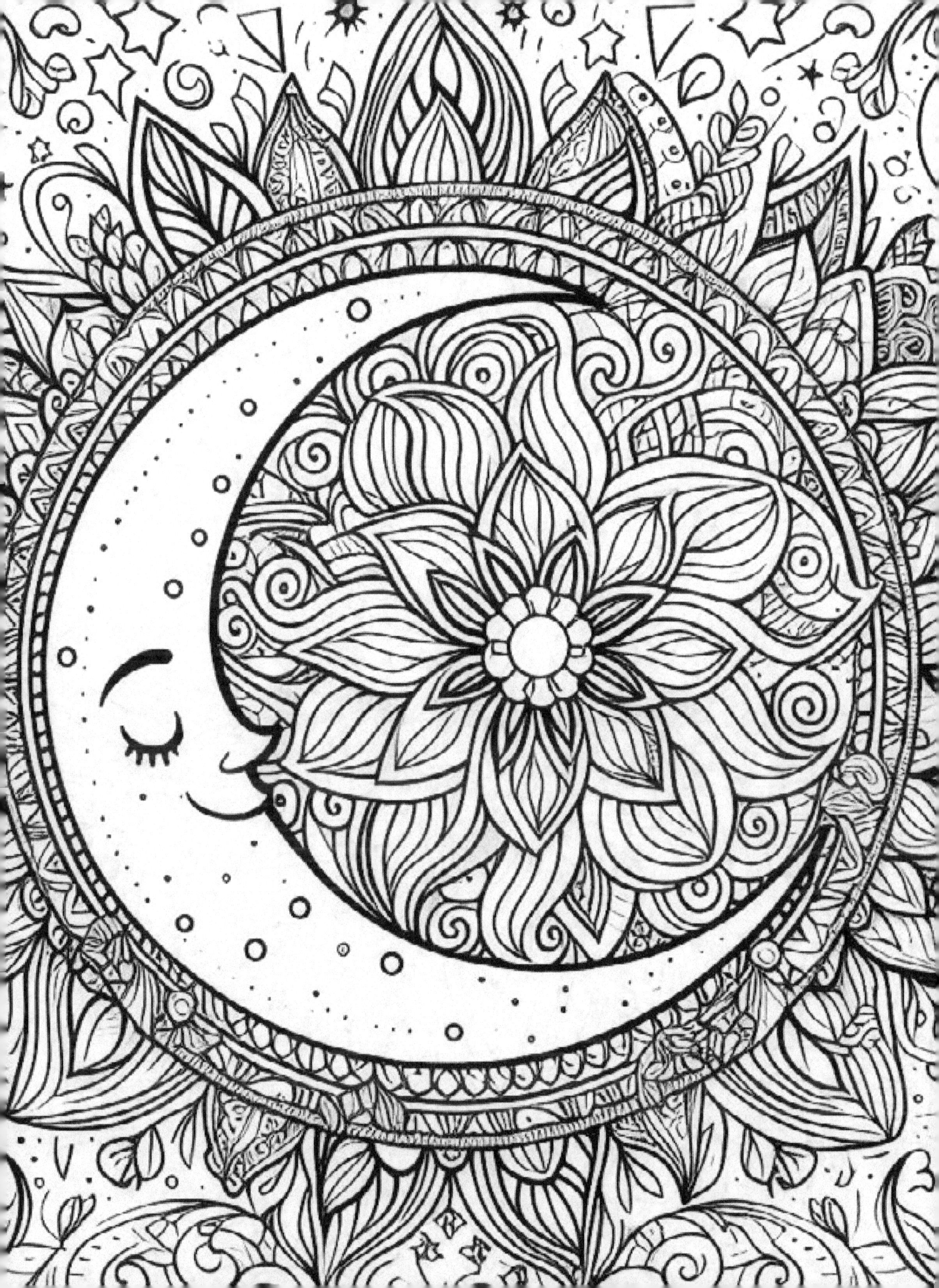

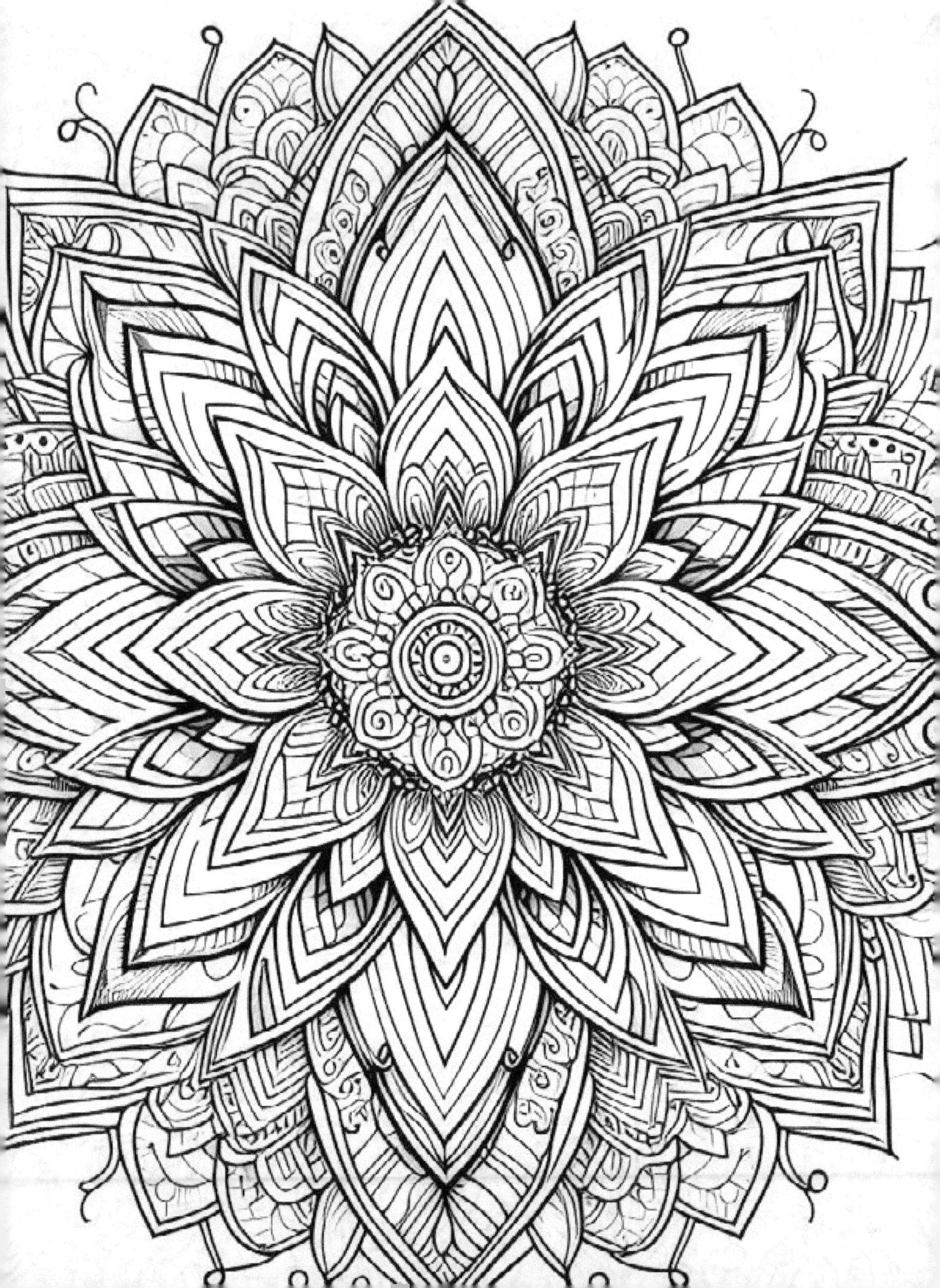

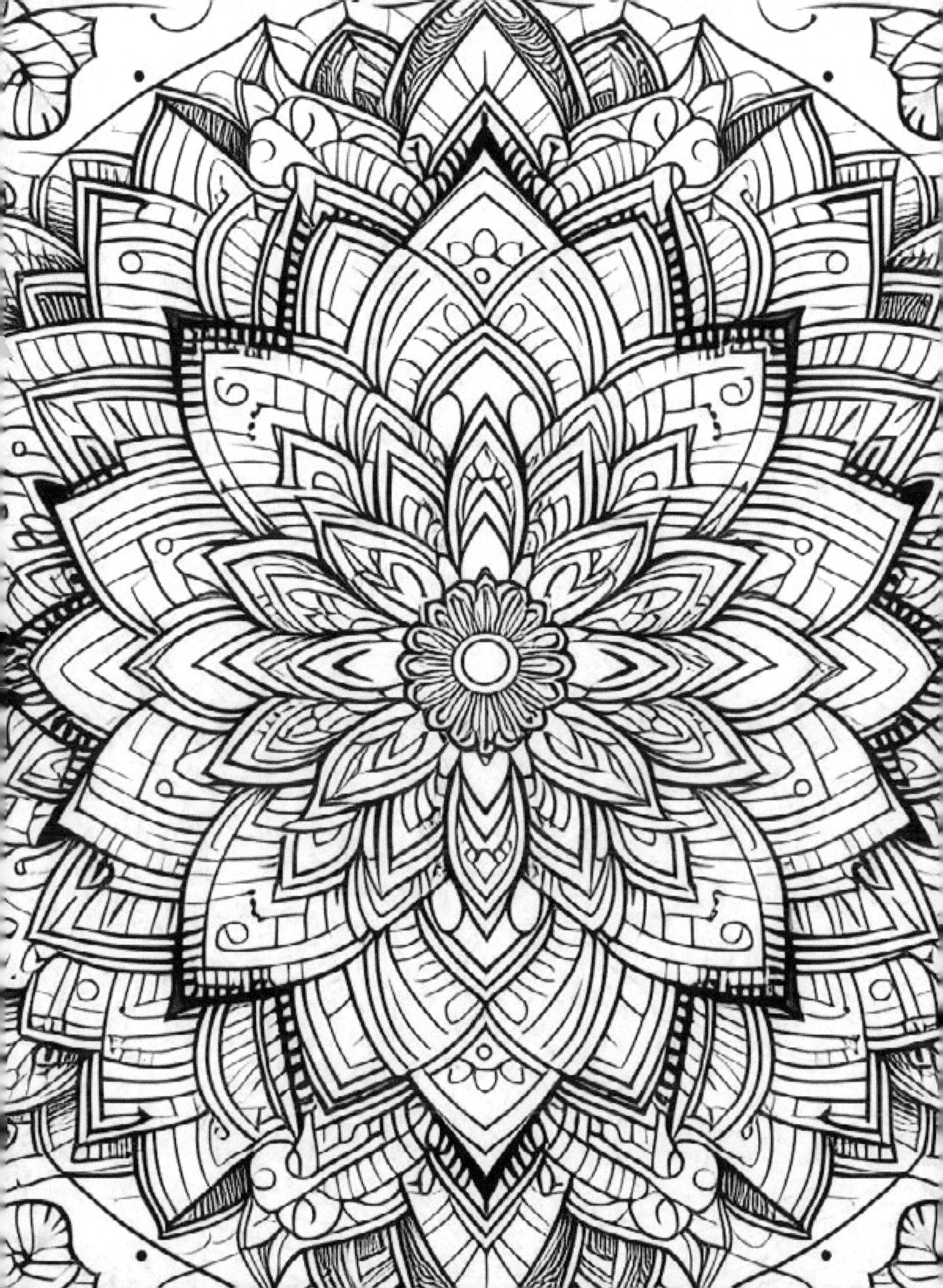

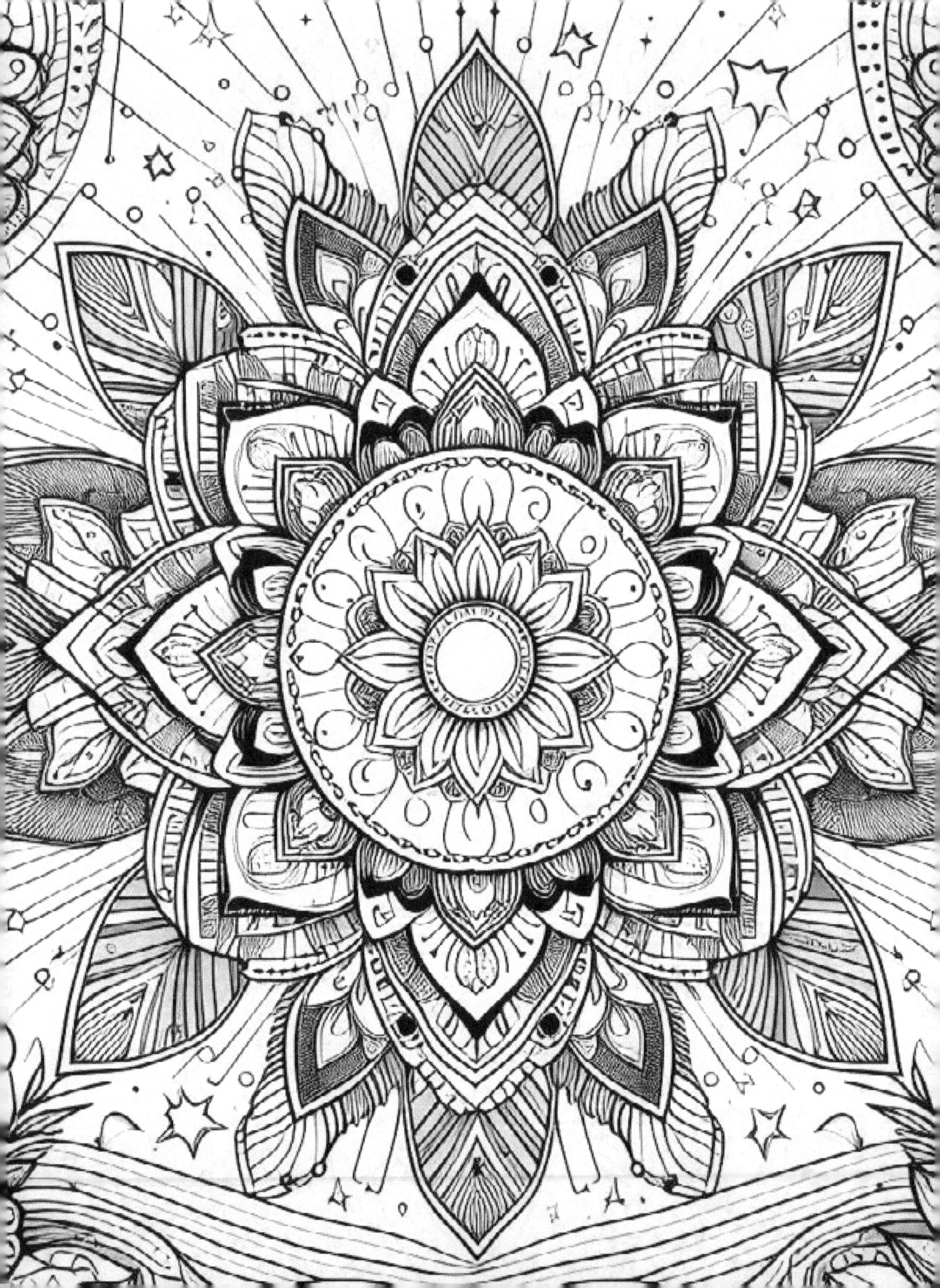

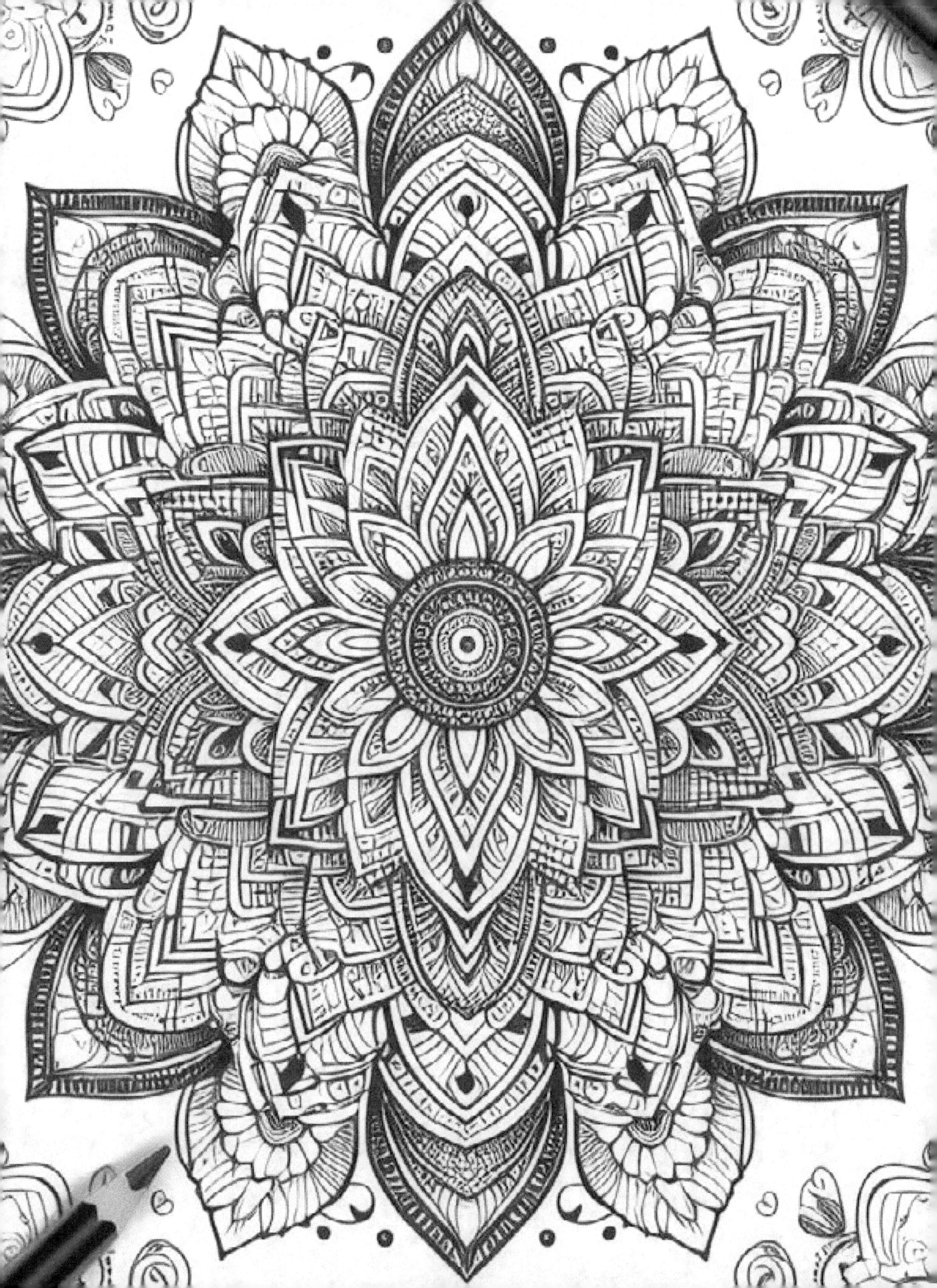

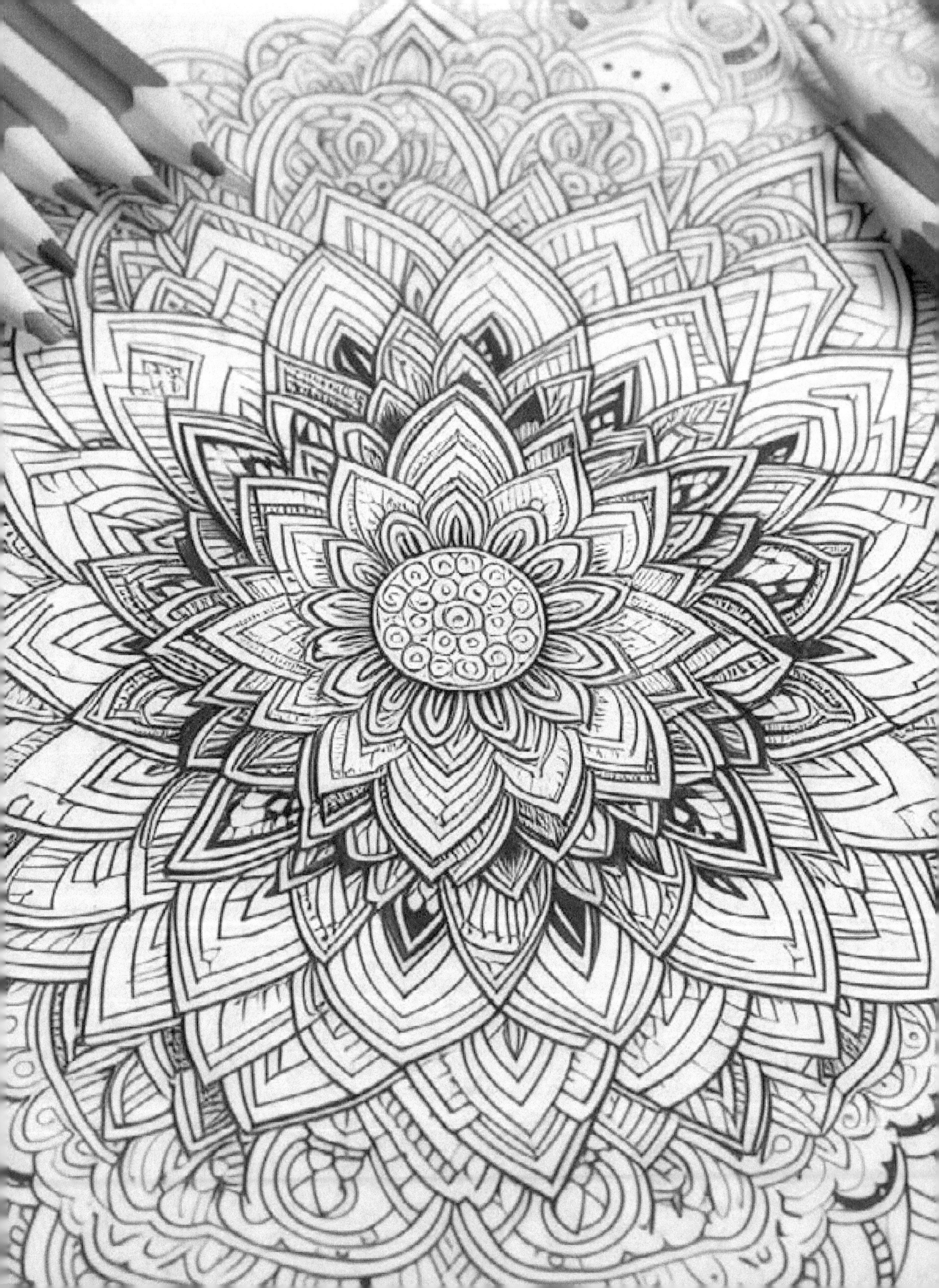

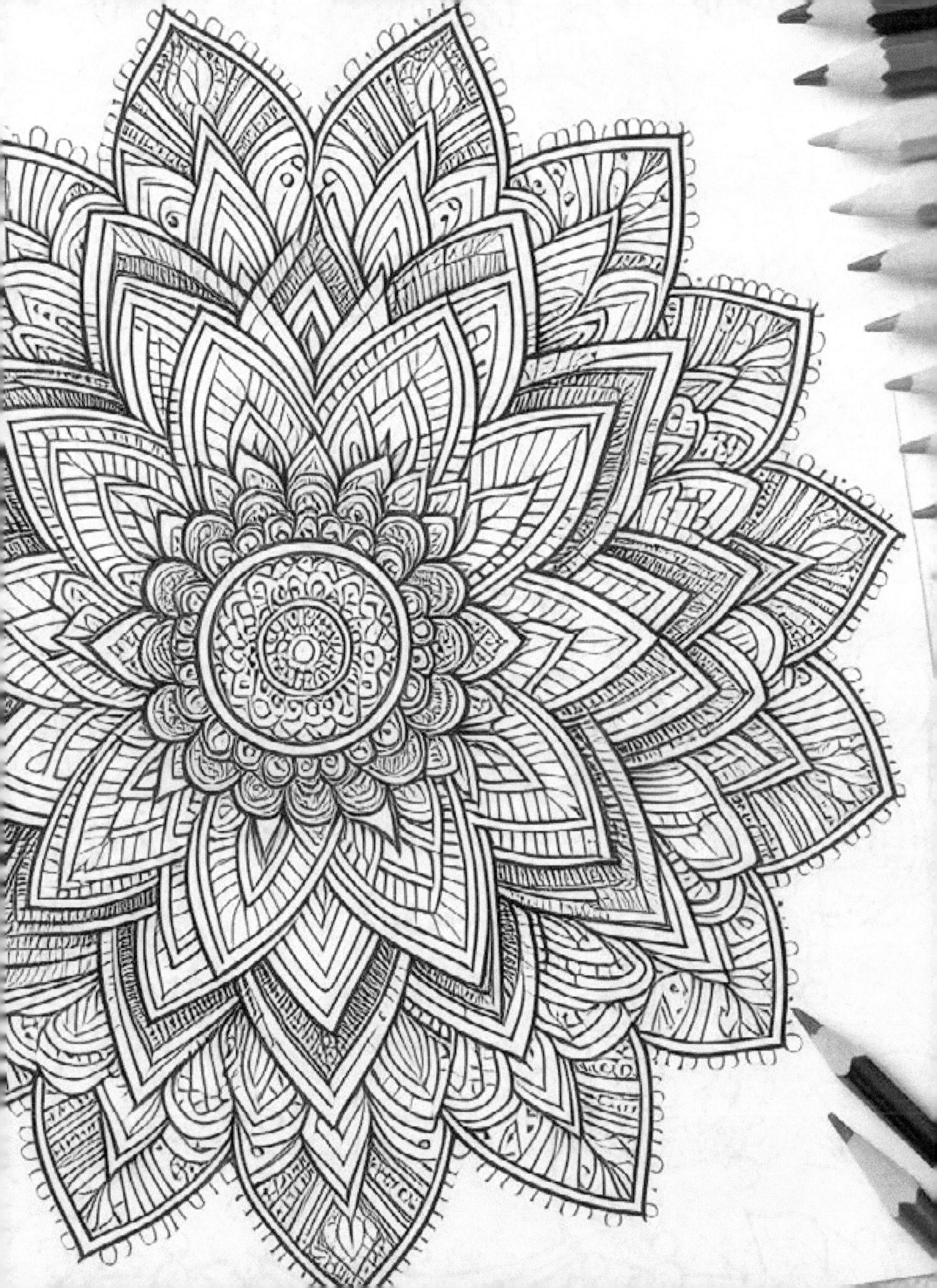

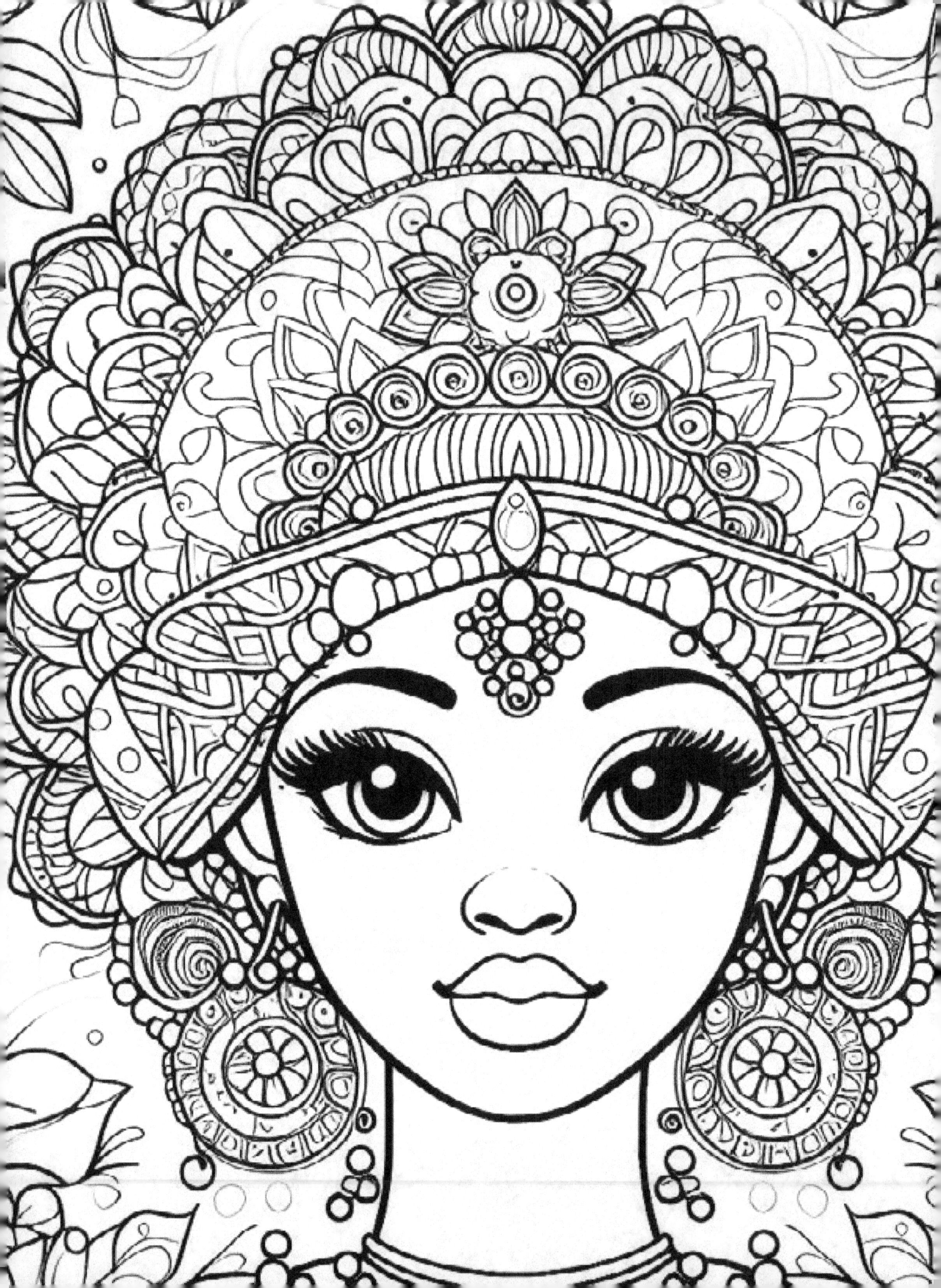

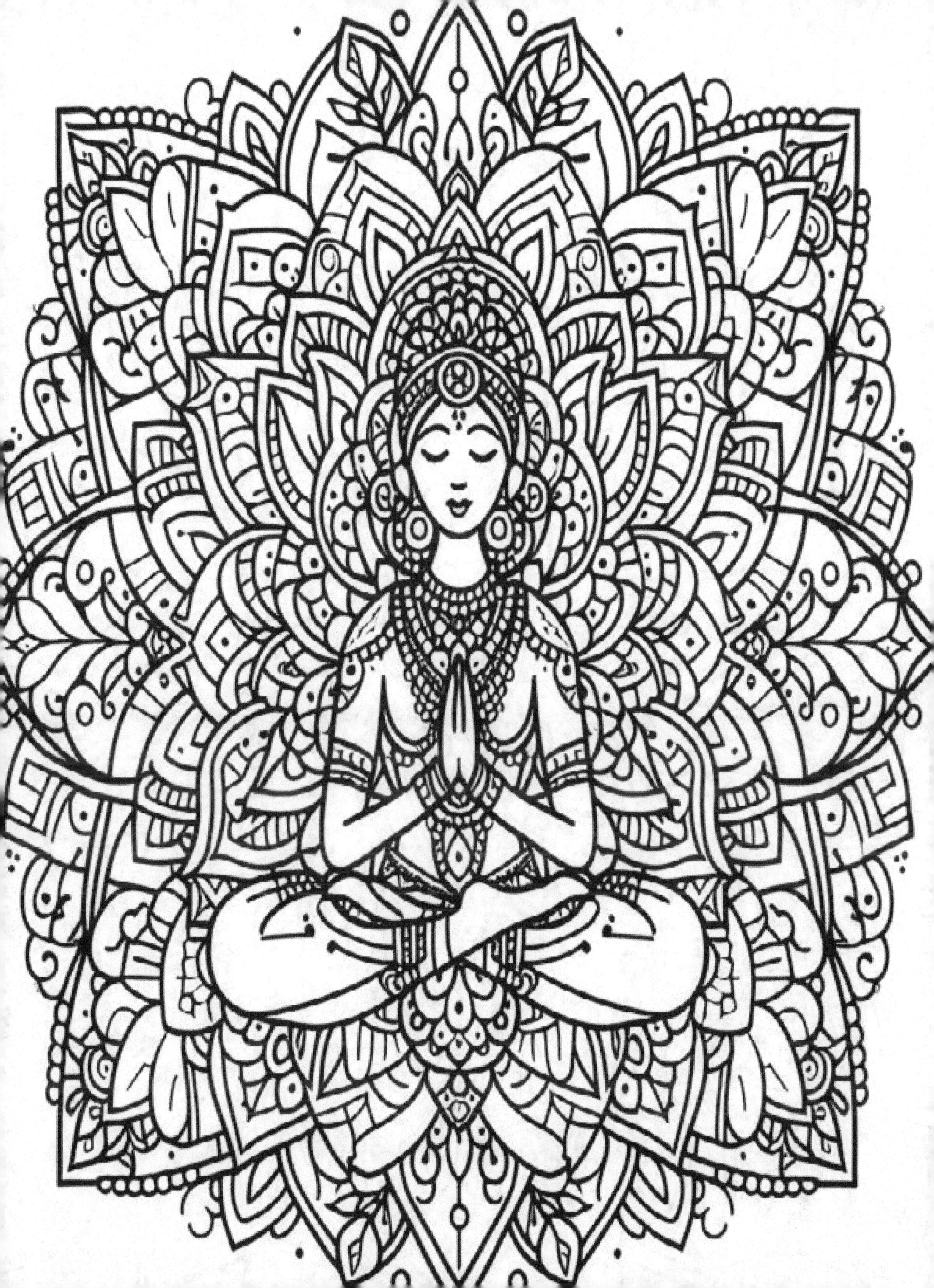

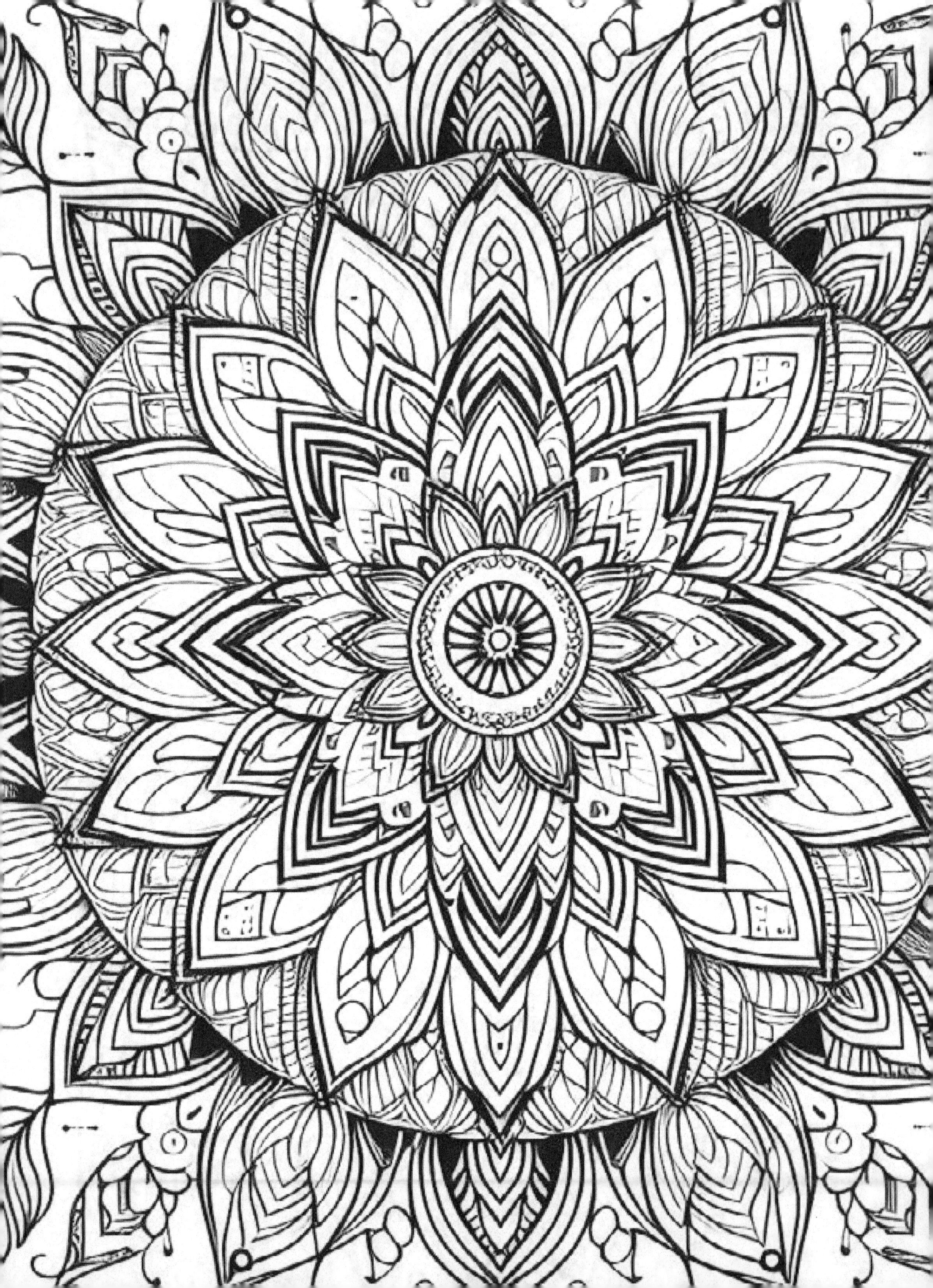

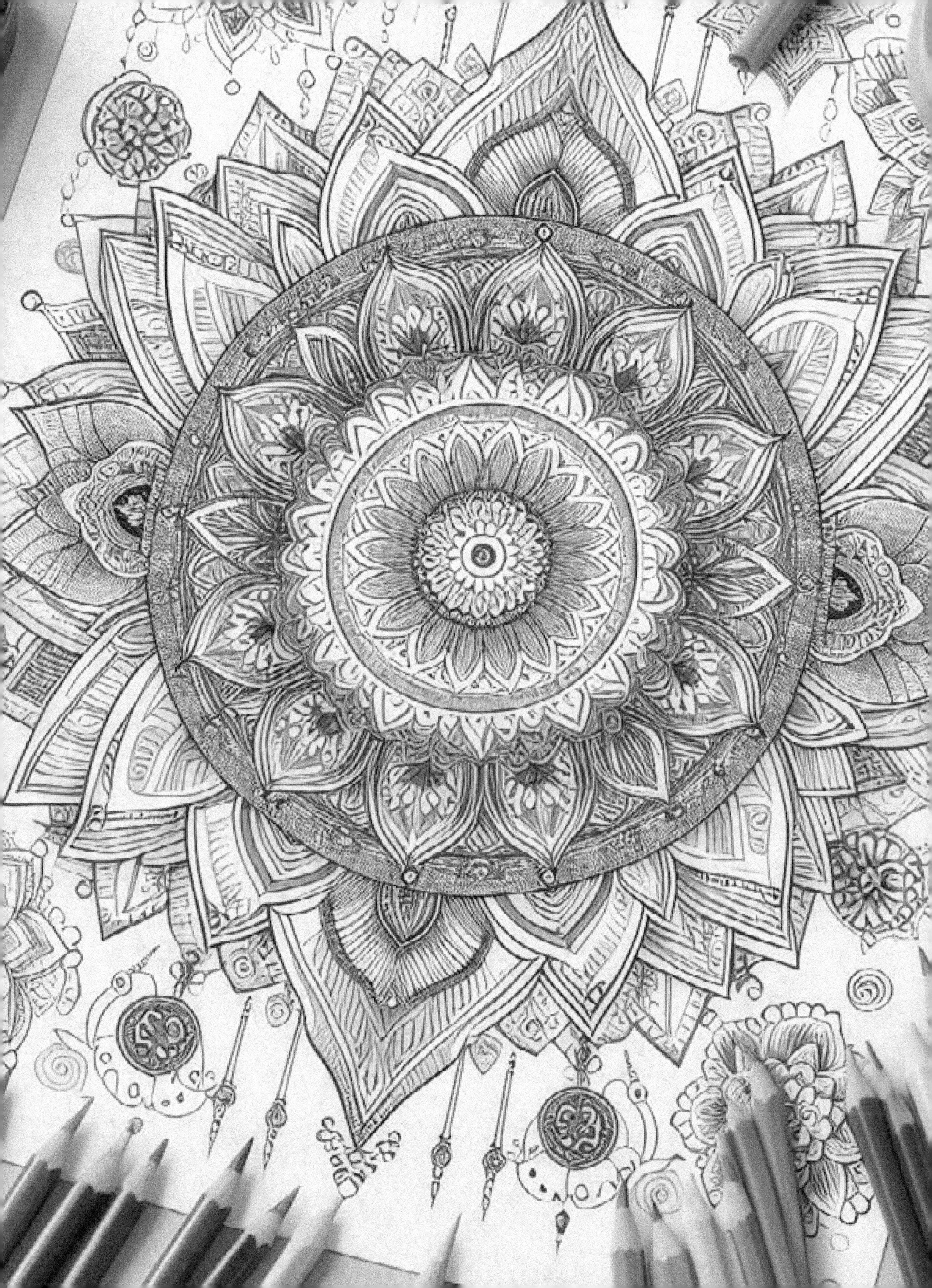

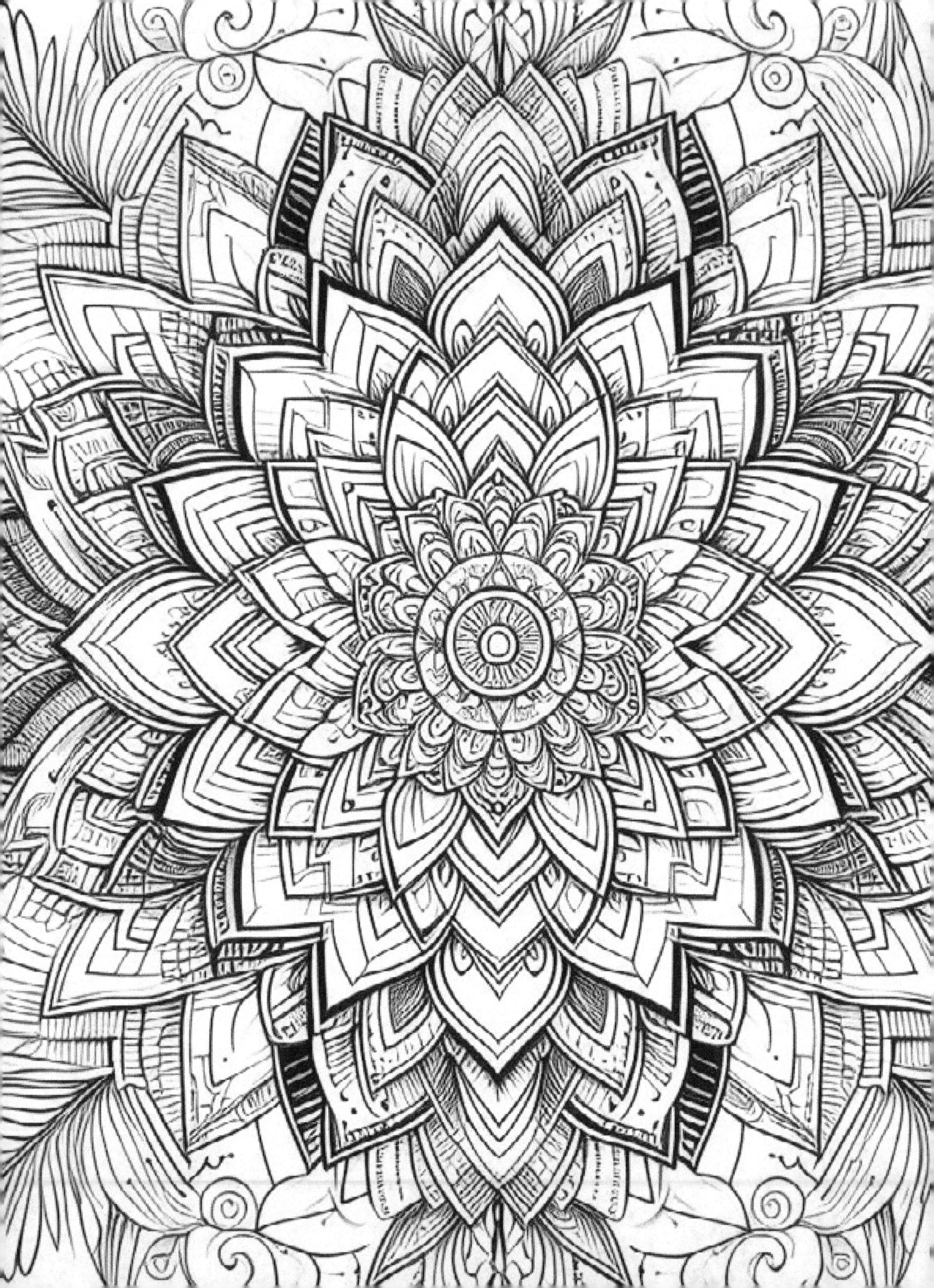

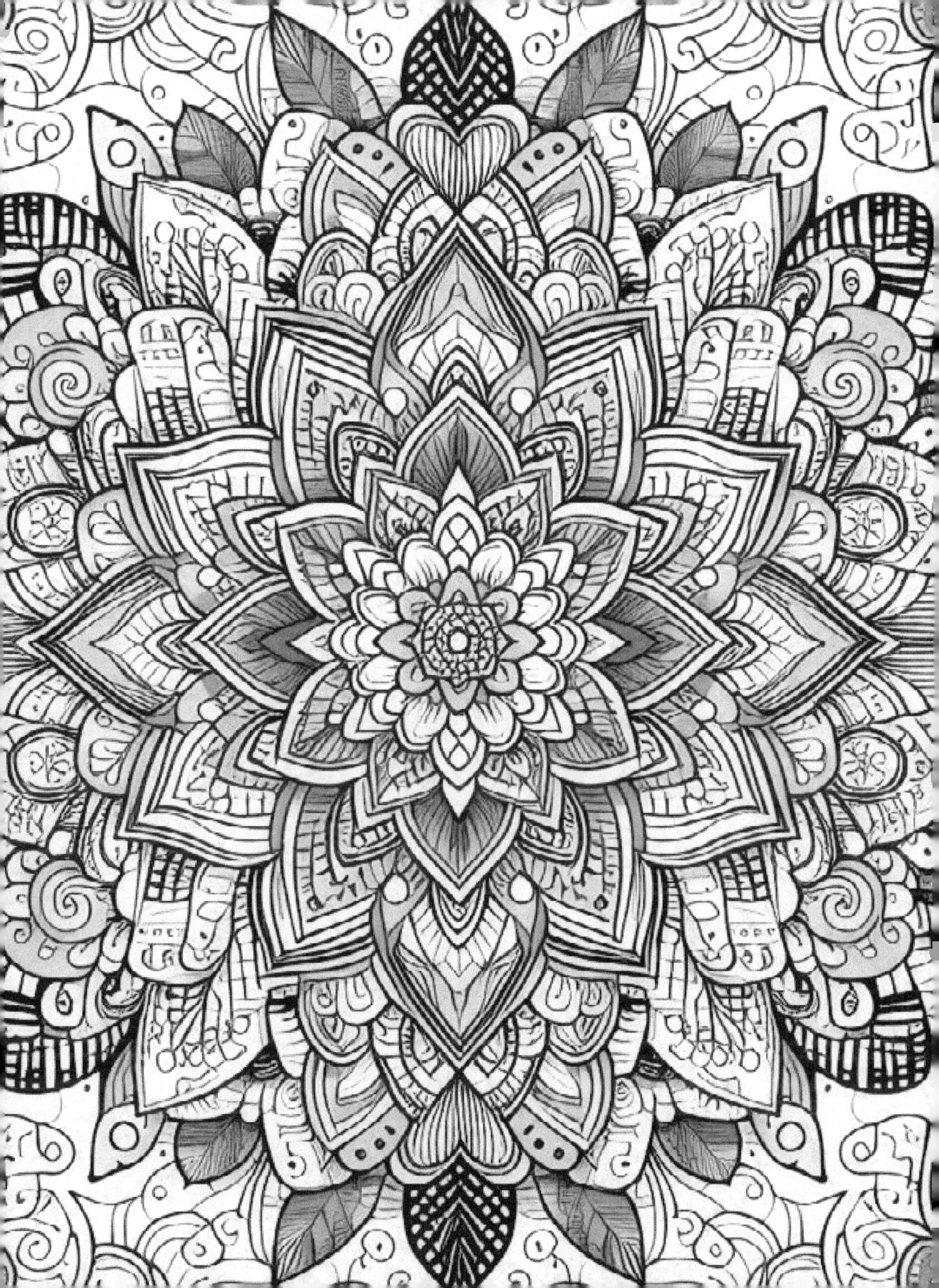

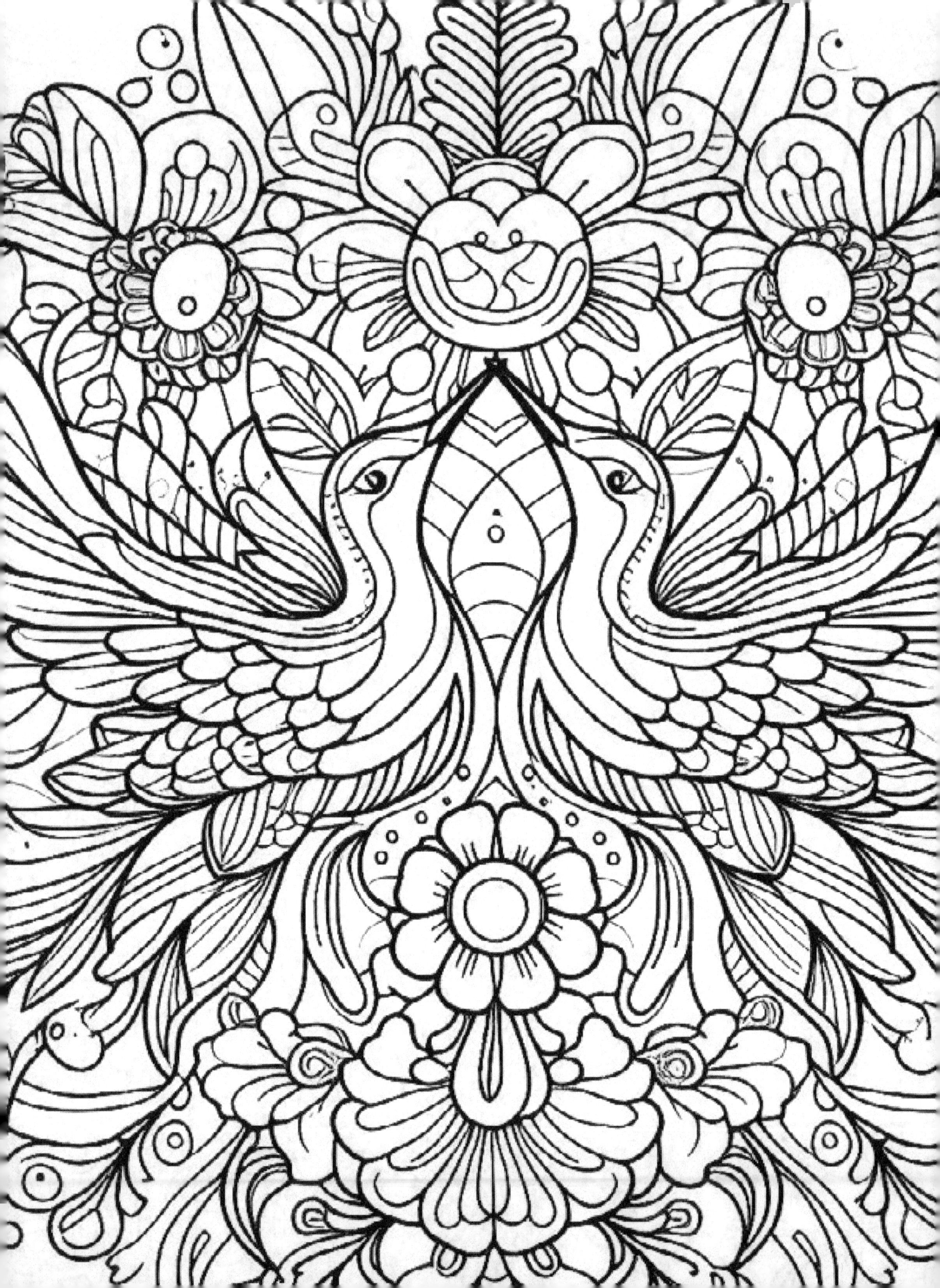

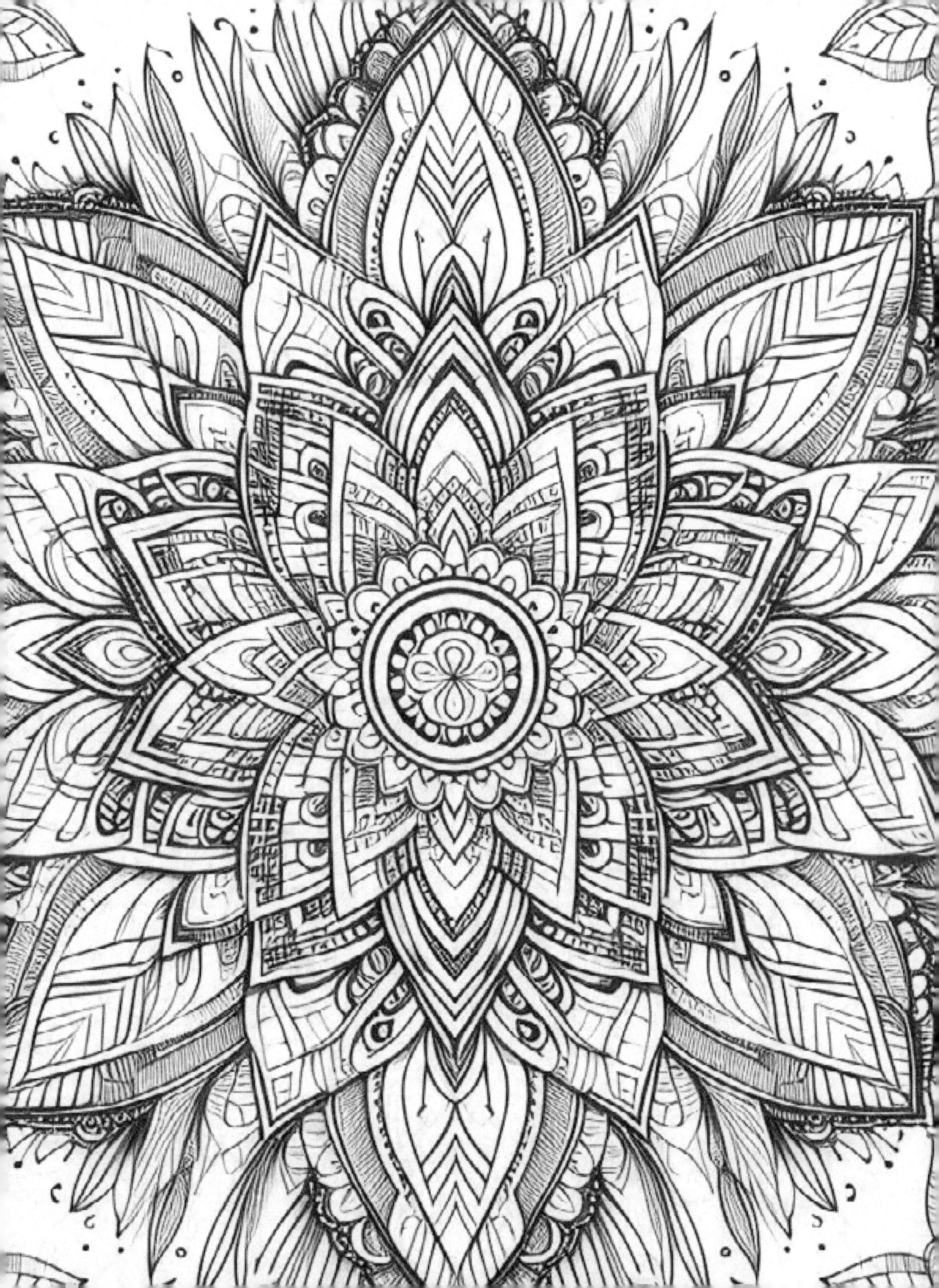

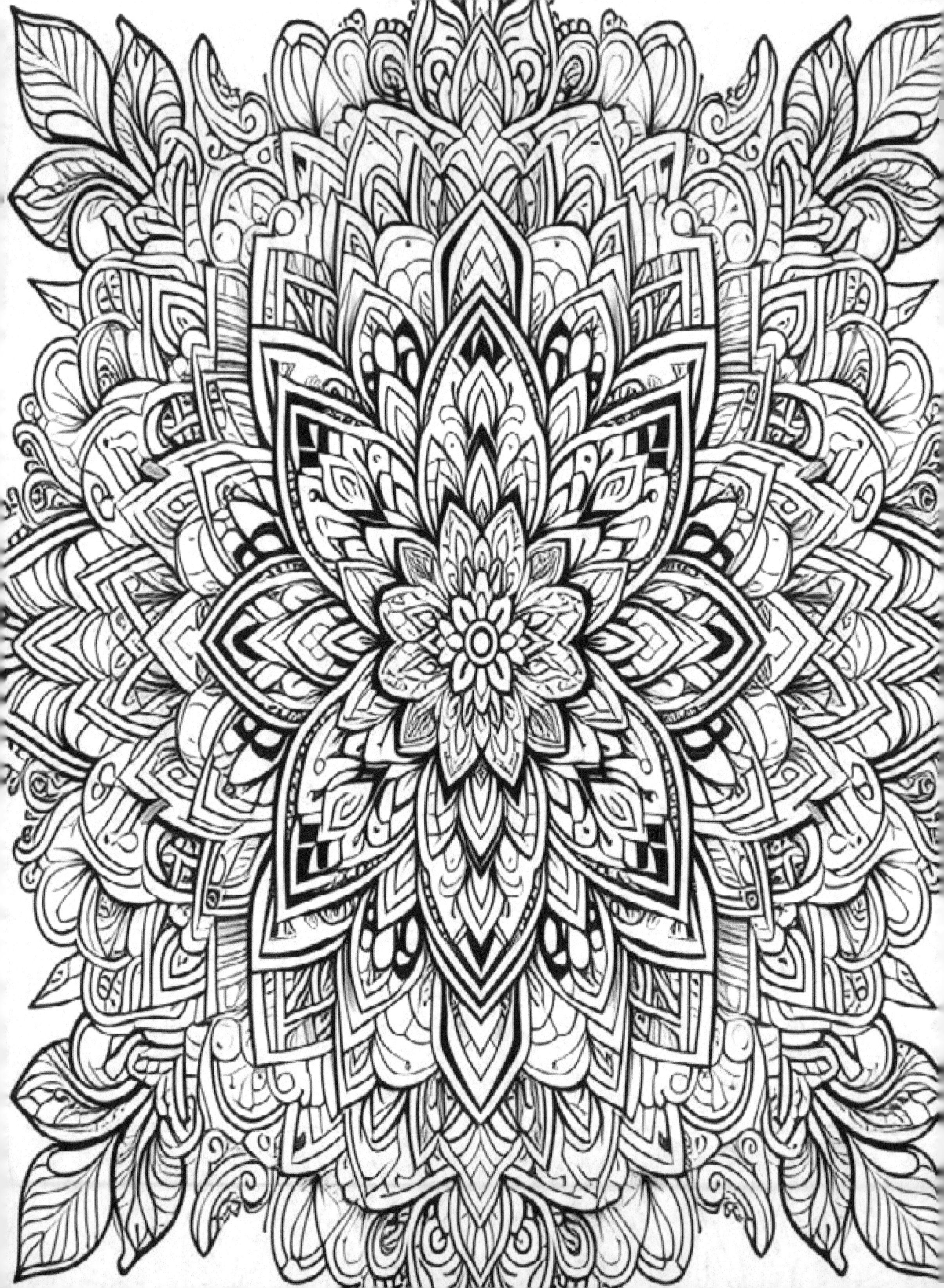

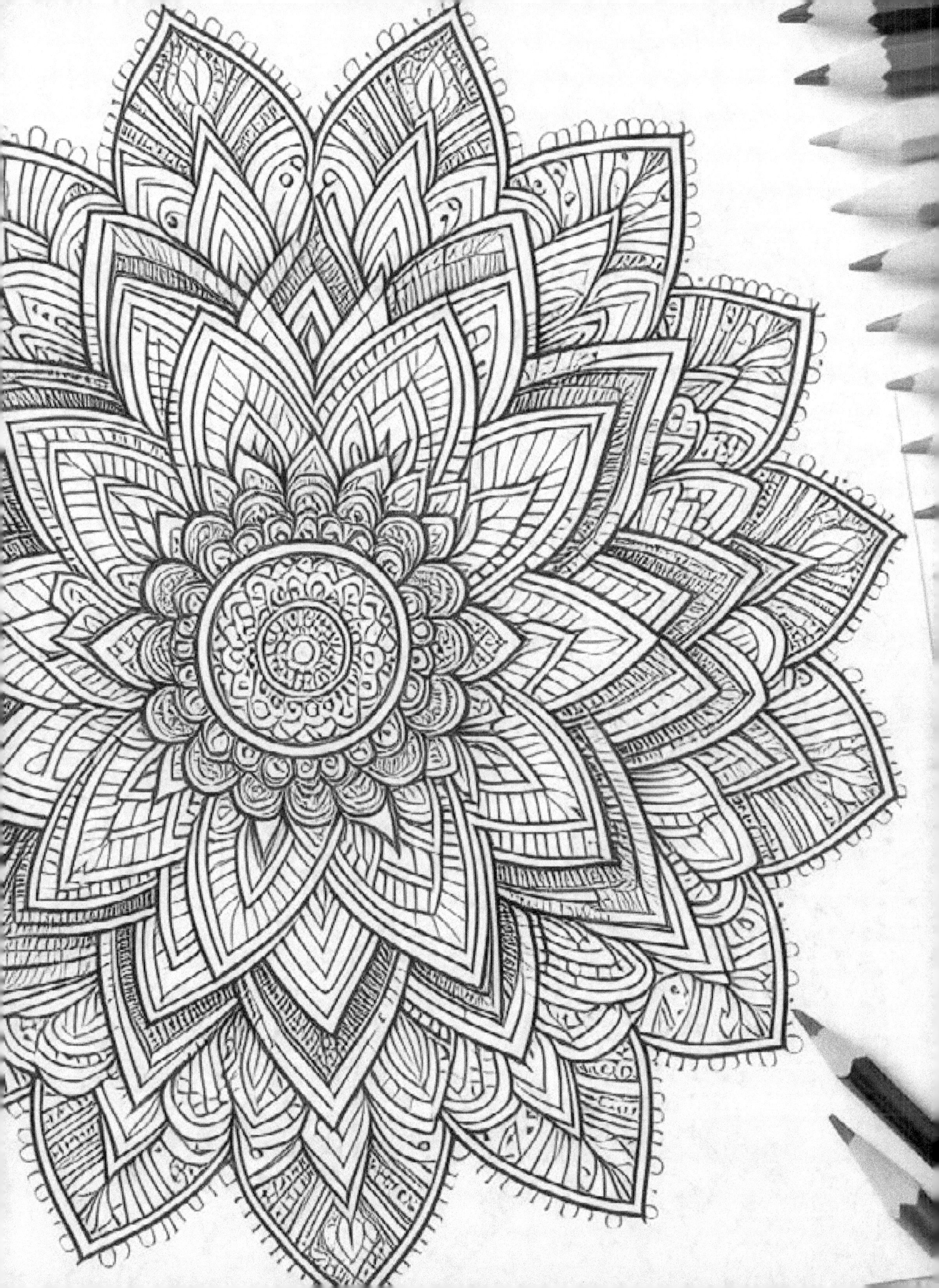

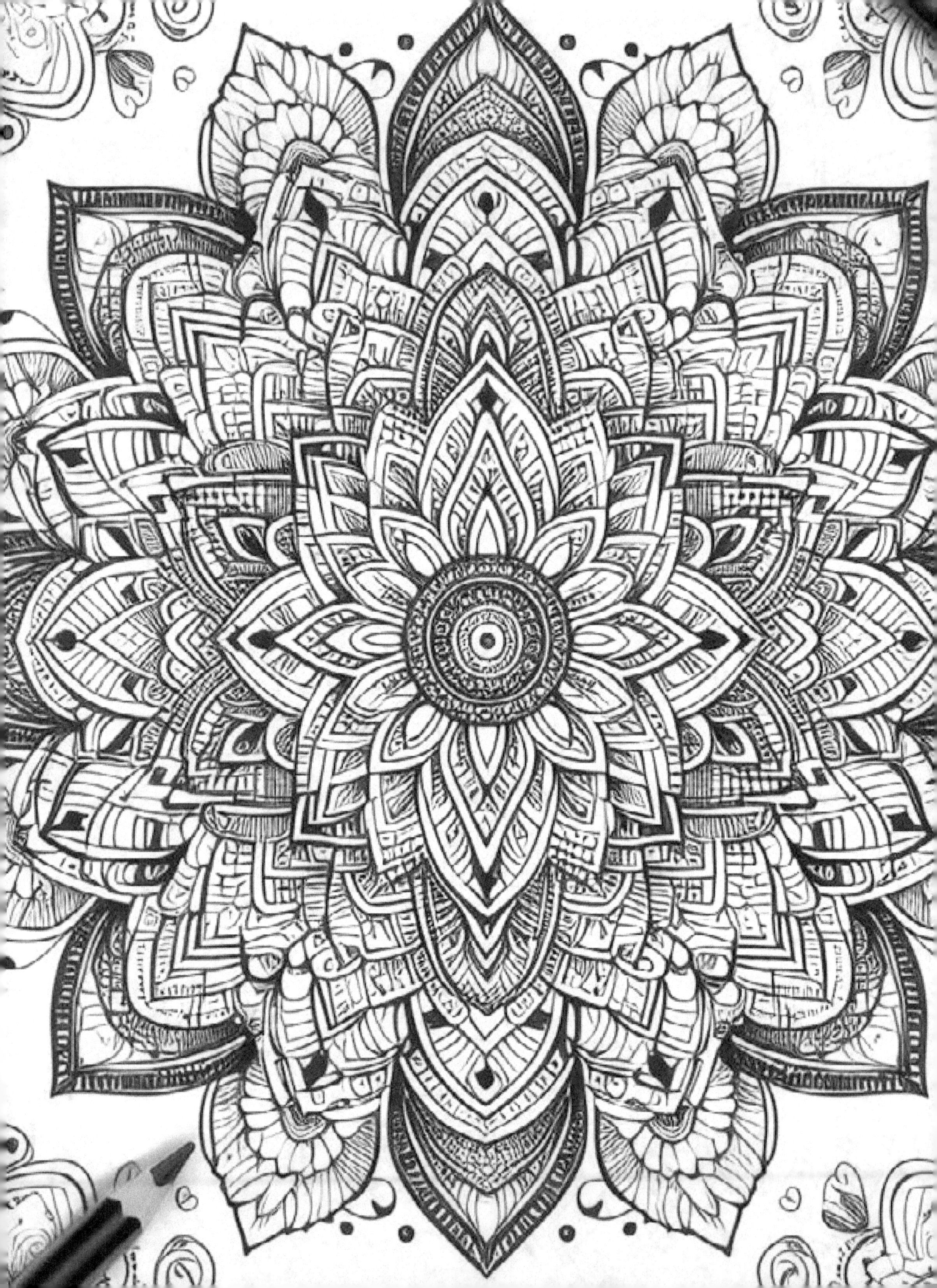

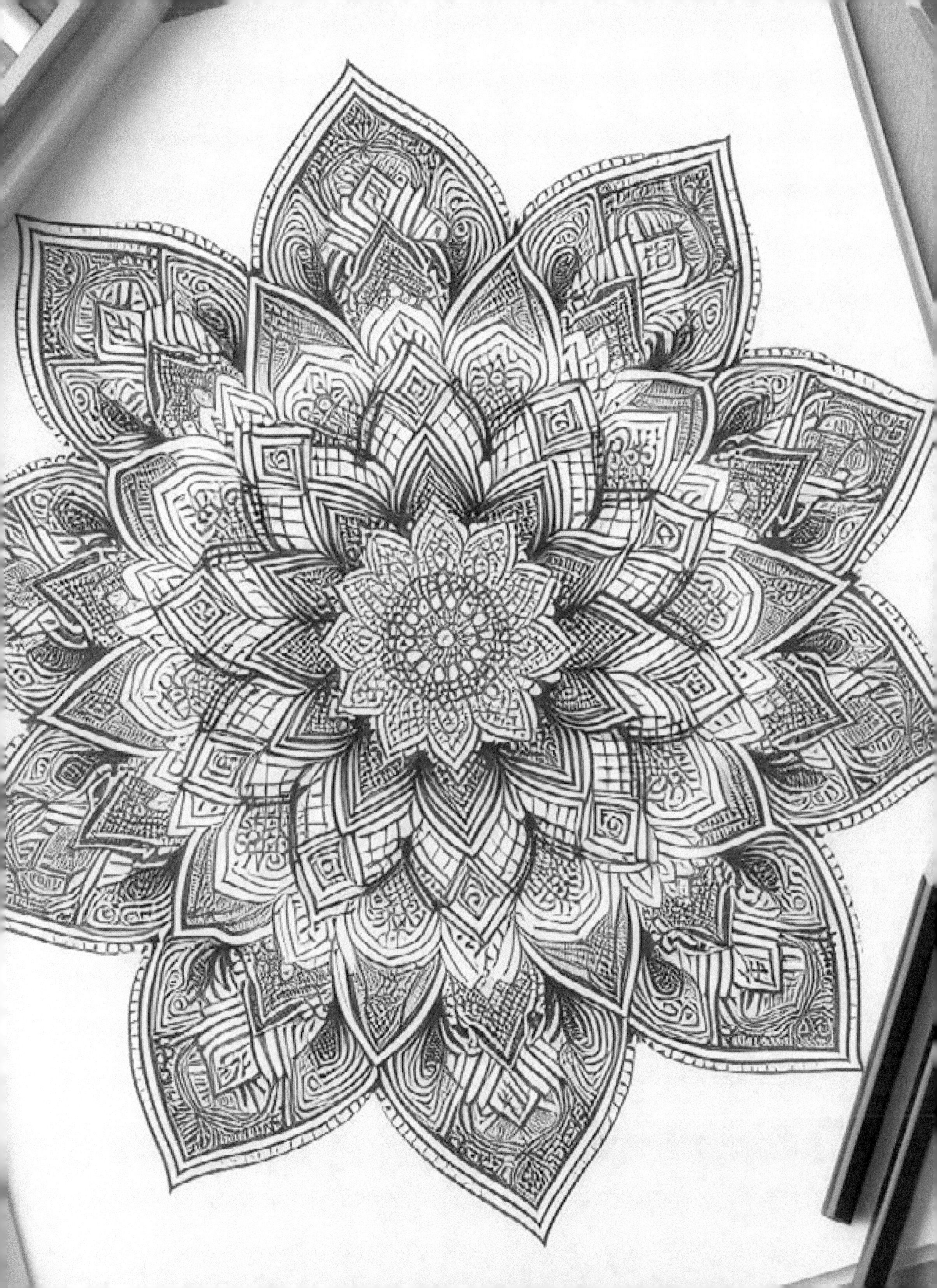